A Little Book of

Sufi Stories

Ancient Wisdom to Nourish the Heart

A Little Book of

Sufi Stories

Ancient Wisdom to Nourish the Heart

NEIL DOUGLAS-KLOTZ

Foreword by MARYAM MAFI

Cover design by Jim Warner
Cover illustration © Kumquat, 1996 (w/c on paper), Eden, Margaret Ann (Contemporary Artist) / Private Collection / Bridgeman Images
Interior by Maureen Forys, Happenstance Type-O-Rama
Typeset in Mrs. Eaves and Mrs. Eaves XL Serif Narrow

Hampton Roads Publishing Company, Inc.
Charlottesville, VA 22906
Distributed by Red Wheel/Weiser, LLC
www.redwheelweiser.com

ISBN: 978-1-57174-829-4
Library of Congress Cataloging-in-Publication Data available upon request.

Printed in Canada
MAR
10 9 8 7 6 5 4 3 2 1

For Sauluddin—friend, spiritual mentor,
living Sufi, master of the magic words:
"Once upon a time . . . it just so happened. . . ."

Contents

Foreword

"Somebody please give us some good news!" blasted the loudspeakers at St. Paul's Cathedral in June 2017 in London as the ordination ceremony began. The good reverend could not have been more to the point as he addressed those of us who had gathered to celebrate the young and the not-so-young men and women who were going to devote the rest of their lives to spiritual pursuit.

We do indeed live in precarious times, when "good news" seems but a vain hope, but our situation is by no means unique. Circumstances have been more uncertain and dangerous in the past, and we have survived them and our story continues. In fact, life is a series of successive stories, often long and winding with endlessly changing expectations and surprises. Everything we experience in our lives harbors a story; every thought and creation, every endeavor—be it artistic or scientific, literary or musical, pertaining to film or the visual arts or sports—everything we conceive of has a backstory worth knowing, and that is what real life is made of.

Those stories most worthy of our attention are universal and timeless, and although they may change form, subject, or language, they succeed in maintaining the pure essence of the original thought; therefore, they are immediately familiar to us. Sufi stories fit this description; irrespective of language and culture, they are ageless, filled with age-old wisdom that in the mad rush of modern life we often lose sight of. These stories are rooted in the fundamental elements of life, commonsense issues that we face daily—but so fleeting is our attention, so fickle is our interest, that we're often left unprepared to tackle even the most mundane events simply because we can't find answers to our questions on Google or Wikipedia. Time has become more ephemeral than ever before as we are exposed to panoramas of random phenomena through social media. We go online, and before we know it, hours have passed while we were switching from Facebook to Instagram to Twitter and other sites. Were we inspired in any way? The answer for many will certainly be a resounding "yes," but for most of us the reality is likely another story.

Sufi stories are like ancient historical sites that require mindful preservation and upkeep; we need to be always reminded of the brilliance that created them, and the insight and wisdom that they continue to deliver are essential for future generations. Historical sites from all cultural and spiritual heritages are critical tools that allow us to access our past and gain insight into our origins, achievements, and contributions. When we find ourselves in the presence of an ancient monument, we are touched deeply in our consciousness in that place where we share oneness with all other people—our human heritage. It is the same when we hear a Sufi story for the first time.

Storytelling—one of the earliest modes of human communication—remains to this day one of the most powerful ways of connecting our souls with one another. Retelling classical Sufi stories from various traditions in modern English is a priceless service that Neil Douglas-Klotz here offers his readers. He has included many humorous stories in this collection, and indeed one of the inherent and essential elements of most Sufi stories is humor (undoubtedly a quality we could all use a little more of in today's world!). Humor is an especially valuable ingredient in that it helps draw us, and our children, into these parables of ancient wisdom, stories that may otherwise be off-putting or difficult to digest. With his masterful interpretive storytelling, not only does Douglas-Klotz impart Sufi wisdom without adopting a patronizing attitude, but he also interjects little gems of his own humor in exactly the right instances, successfully keeping our attention honed. To hear Nassrudin Hoja's hysterically funny instructional stories spreading from Ottoman Turkey across Persian lands all the way to the khanates of central Asia, literally thousands of miles apart, conveys the reality that our borders are only imaginary and that human beings everywhere have always been one and the same.

Douglas-Klotz points out how Carl Jung and other archetypal psychologists have tried to classify folktales according to various theories about the human personality, which can be done in various ways. However, Sufi stories should be allowed, as he reminds us, to stand for themselves, and we must leave them to do their work on their own, which they have achieved quite well through the centuries and without the aid of psychologists. If we could only read them without applying our modern-day logic, without categorizing or compartmentalizing them, simply letting them seep into our minds without trying to explain their effect on our psyche, we could benefit from them all the more. Douglas-Klotz depicts corresponding concepts arising from the Judaic, Christian, and Islamic traditions—such as Iblis, the Angel of Death—and refreshingly presents us with interpretations from these various faiths. By doing so, he prompts us to expand our vision, encouraging us to make up our own minds rather than be influenced exclusively by whatever tradition we have been raised in. As he weaves his way in and out of the stories, he offers us prescient explanations at the right moments, guiding us through texts that are seemingly simple yet are multifaceted and spiritually complex.

If you want to hear a good story but prefer to *read* it instead, then read Douglas-Klotz! He writes as if he's sitting in your living room, invited over for afternoon tea to entertain you with some heart-pleasing, often humorous, yet soul-searching Sufi stories. His modernization of these old texts is gentle and mindful, yet unapologetic. Not all stories portray the Sufis in a positive light, and they often don't end as one would expect; sometimes the villains go unpunished, sometimes the lovers remain separated, and sometimes when lovers are reunited they later realize what a big mistake they've made—all true-to-life scenarios. However, it's imperative to pay attention to what might be happening in a different corner of our minds while we're reading these stories. Their ultimate purpose, after all, is to change and broaden our understanding of the world outside, and more importantly to sharpen our attentiveness to what is actually happening to our world inside.

—*Maryam Mafi*, author of *Rumi's Little Book of Life*

Introduction

We have so many things to engage our attention these days: twenty-four-hour rolling news, social networks, online animal videos, multiplex films, stand-up comedians, and postmodern performance art. You might ask: is there any room left for the humble Sufi story?

First, let's deal with our culture's obsession with news and "facts." As the great American storyteller Mark Twain once said, there are three categories of untruth: lies, damn lies, and statistics. When I worked as a journalist forty years ago, it was clear even then that reporters on the scene could have their work selectively edited to present quite a different story from what an eyewitness would have experienced. And as we experience every day, different people see and remember different things. Even video can be edited. As distinguished from facts, alternative facts, and news, the Sufi story presents us with something else: true fiction. These timeless stories reveal something very deep about the way we experience and create different realities out of the stuff of life.

As to our engagement with the entertainment industry, the Sufi story cannot, of course, compete with the special effects of the digital age. But a Sufi teacher telling a story never sets out to simply perform or entertain. Each telling of a story is unique, each interwoven with a tapestry of local relationship and meaning that we might today call a spiritual community, even when it forms spontaneously. Within this community, a mutual search for wisdom demands that the storyteller respond to the moment, not give a rehearsed performance. When mystics and students gather, the teacher intersperses stories with spiritual practices or meditation that lead them all to the doorway of an experience that reframes one's ordinary sense of reality. But showing someone a gate is different from a person going through that gate—hence the need for stories to offer an added, gentle push.

Yet if mere self-improvement were the goal, why tell stories when we have so many valuable self-help methods to transform our psyche and consciousness? The further we go into the "self," the more we find that logical systems don't help very much. Most of life doesn't obey even the most complex algorithms that artificial intelligence can conceive (witness the ups and downs of the stock market if you doubt this). When a Sufi tells a story, no PowerPoint is used, no bullet-pointed thought nuggets conveyed to be studiously notated. These stories cannot be diced, sliced, parsed, or interpreted for their metaphoric or allegorical meaning. In fact, if you tell a Sufi story well, to interpret it would kill it. If I tell you that such and such a character means this, the bird is the soul, the donkey is our ego, blah, blah, blah . . . it's all nonsense.

Like a Zen koan, a real Sufi story allows a person's innate wisdom to arise from the inside. And wisdom (unlike its poor cousin, the fact or supposed fact) cannot be given like a pill to the merely rational, cognitive side of our minds. That part of our mind—useful in many situations—fixates on a supposed meaning, ideal, or principle, and then strolls away happily, completely unchanged in its depths.

In those depths lie all the important feelings, inklings, habits, and passions that control most of our lives. When only the modern, surface part of our heart-mind gets involved, even a story told by a Buddha can turn into a tale heard by an idiot, signifying nothing.

Jesus said it best in the Gospels. When asked by his disciples why he didn't simply say clearly what he was talking about, the master responded that one part of our heart-mind can hear things directly—it stays in the territory illuminated by light's straight lines. Another, deeper part lingers in the darkness and understands only by coming to its own realization. To touch that more obscure side of our being, we need to travel a different path: the spiral, serpentine way. So, Jesus recommended that his students use suitable vehicles to get where they're going. Sometimes, he said, go openly and obviously like a dove, and at other times, travel like a serpent, writhing through the night in secret. (This saying is usually translated as "Be wise as serpents and tender as doves.")

Traveling in this wiggle-waggle way, a Sufi story arises from the inspired depths of wisdom that give birth to all the great stories of humanity. In the ancient Middle East, the Semitic prophets connected this path with the figure of Holy Wisdom or Sophia, with whom many of his early followers associated Jesus. In response to life's deeper conundrums, this storytelling, wisdom-way can change a *hah?* into an *aha!*

Rather than add to our storehouse of learned information, these stories help us "unlearn" and break down the neurotic, mental-emotional patterns that protect our false sense of who we are. As we go beyond these boundaries, we may find ourselves in the province of wild nature. We discover an inner landscape, less controlled yet richer than that of our self-imposed rules for life. In this sense, these stories function almost exactly opposite to the computer algorithms of social media, which feed back to us things that reinforce what we already like (or think we like).

As the German novelist and storyteller Hermann Hesse once wrote, the great stories of humanity—like fairy tales, Hasidic stories, Celtic stories, Zen stories, and Sufi stories—provide us with incomparable examples of the "genetic history of the soul." We share this depth of soul with all human beings. So, hearing a story *live* and unrehearsed brings us closer together, creating and re-creating our all-too-fragile sense of human community.

Sources of the Stories

I have drawn the stories in this book from the dozens that I have enjoyed telling in my teaching seminars over the past thirty-plus years. Most of them first appear in works of classical Sufis like Rumi, Attar, or Sa'adi. Others simply come to us without a name, passed down from person to person with variations for hundreds of years.

Telling an oral story in print is challenging. One can strip the story back to its bare bones, thereby losing much of its flavor and aroma. Or one can treat the story like a prehistoric insect caught in amber: one leaves all sorts of cultural detail in, but the story doesn't breathe. I am a great fan of live storytellers, but some so-called professional storytellers err on the latter side, because they don't understand the transmission of the story—its life as an inner experience that everyone can share. The "wow" factor may be there—the special effects—but not the wisdom.

Likewise, some authors overly embellish or interpret Sufi stories with an agenda in mind (often psychological or theological). They map out the whole story as an allegory that supports a principle they want to convey. In my view, this is (as one Zen master commented) like going to a restaurant and ordering a vitamin pill. Where is the art of life, the joy of discovery?

Hopefully, I have woven my way between the extremes. I have modernized the dialogue, and so there will be deliberately anachronistic references. Hint: This is one technique for using stories as spiritual teaching. Another technique: There will be plot elements that seem to end nowhere. A third: No "trigger warnings" are given. Fourth: Sometimes the good are not rewarded and the evil not punished (but that's more like life anyway). I could go on, but why spoil the fun?

As I mentioned, a Sufi storyteller will often intersperse the story with meditation, spiritual practice, prayer, or teaching. The famous 13th-century Sufi Jelaluddin Rumi does this in his long epic poem titled the *Mathnawi* (the name of the verse form). One needs to read these stories in their complete form to understand how Rumi weaves his spell. The "stray threads" he introduces may seem like digressions, but they function more like a magician's sleight of hand. When you're looking in one direction, something else is happening within you. To achieve some of this in print, I have offered cultural commentary or asides in the middle of some stories.

Without doubt, there is nothing like hearing a Sufi story live. To tell one of these stories, I need to first live in it for a while, much as one might walk into an unknown forest and gradually get to know the plants and animals there. Yet when telling the story live, I can still meet something unexpected at any moment.

As I mentioned in *The Sufi Book of Life* (Penguin Books, 2005), I encourage readers to go beyond the book (or screen) to meet real Sufis. With a sincere heart, this is not so hard (which is not to say it's simple, given that Sufis all over the world are under threat from Islamic fundamentalists).

I hope these stories convey an aliveness that awakens a spark in your soul. If they do, you may become—as I am—a story collector.

Hear and read more of them, retell them in your own way, and you may find yourself becoming a different, wilder, more completely human *you*.

—Neil Douglas-Klotz
(Saadi Shakur Chishti)
Fife, Scotland
May 2017

A Little Book of

Sufi Stories

Ancient Wisdom to Nourish the Heart

The Stories

I

Stories about Sufis and Dervishes

You might think that Sufi stories always portray Sufis in a positive light. But you would be thinking incorrectly.

One famous story, told by the 12th-century Sufi Fariduddin Attar, relates that a Sufi shaykh was once traveling on the back of a donkey, congratulating himself for being such a wise teacher with so many students. Then his donkey farts. This "Zen moment" occasions sincere repentance on the part of the shaykh, who feels that his *nafs*, or small self, has just made an apt commentary on his self-worth.

Rumi relates our first story in his *Mathnawi*, a long poetic opus of about 25,000 verses, often informally called the "Persian Qur'an." Several of Rumi's stories deal with the challenges and foibles of Sufi dervishes during his time.

The second story comes from Ottoman Turkey. You could see it merely as a satire skewering both intellectuals and dervishes. But let it settle a bit, and you may find something deeper.

The Shaykh and the Boy Selling Halvah

Once upon a time, a famous Sufi shaykh lived in old Baghdad. The shaykh was renowned for his charity and goodness. Aside from what he really needed, he gave away everything he received each day to the poor. So, his reputation among the common folk was outstanding. Almost everyone loved him. Almost.

There was only one problem. Since he didn't own anything, he borrowed everything that he gave away each day. So the shaykh was constantly in debt to many people. Usually some generous person came to his aid whenever he really needed it, but nonetheless he was always only one step ahead of his creditors.

The shaykh was getting on in years, and just as things are today, people became less and less willing to loan him anything for fear that he might not be able to pay them back. Nonetheless, the shaykh's good reputation ensured that there were always people who would loan him what he needed. If nothing else, rich merchants were afraid to let it be known that they were too stingy to give to a generous holy man. It might diminish their customer base.

Now it happened that the shaykh fell ill. And, day by day, he seemed to be failing. The shaykh asked his *murids* (students) to bring his bed into a small meeting hall in the *khanaqah*, the Sufi gathering place where he and a few students lived. The shaykh told them that he wanted to meet his maker there.

Unlike many such edifices in the ancient Sufi world, this *khanaqah* was a very modest, mud-brick affair. The students' rooms surrounded a central, domed mosque and meeting hall, like a heart with two wings enclosing it.

His students gathered around the shaykh's bed, many of them with long faces, hoping for a final blessing from the great man. The shaykh was smiling beneficently and breathing peacefully. Gradually, word got out of the shaykh's imminent passing, and many other people from the neighborhood began to gather. Among them were the shaykh's many creditors. Instead of a final blessing, the creditors had another object in mind: repayment. They hoped that before the shaykh died, he would manifest some miracle and pay them what he owed.

One of them whispered into the ear of another.

"How much does he owe you?"

"One thousand gold dinars. You?"

"Only 500 silver dirhams, thank God! But it's still enough for me."

The atmosphere in the room was very mixed, to say the least: sadness, hope, expectation, anxiety, and a growing undercurrent of whispering and grumbling.

"If he owed that much to you, why did he also borrow from me?"

"Couldn't he have paid me back with what he borrowed from Ahmed? *He* can afford to lose 600."

"It's incredible! He owes all of us!"

In fact, the room was now overfull, and only the small circle of students around his bed protected the shaykh from the increasingly agitated and growing crowd of creditors who edged nearer and nearer.

The shaykh's breath became more and more refined, until only those nearest him could tell whether he was breathing at all. He motioned for one of his students to come closer.

"What are all these others doing here?" he whispered loudly.

"Master, Allah forgive me, but many of them say that you owe them money."

"Money? Oh, yes, yes . . . probably I do. It's all in Allah's hands."

"What does your master say?" asked one of the creditors in a voice everyone could hear.

"The master says," relayed the student, "that your money is all in Allah's hands."

A loud moan went up from the creditors.

"In Allah's hands? You know what that means!"

"I'm done for!" cried one.

"You? I'll be bankrupt!"

Others also proclaimed their incipient destitution, with increasingly cataclysmic predictions about what would happen to their businesses, their families, the whole community they supported! And so on. They began to fight among themselves about who would be more destitute.

"What are they all talking about?" the shaykh whispered to his nearest student. "This is a house of prayer. It has become increasingly noisy in here."

"Forgive me, Allah, they say that they will be bankrupt."

"No," said the shaykh, "how can it be? I don't believe it. *Ya Alim!* Allah knows the truth."

The students also became increasingly agitated. Not only was this very embarrassing, but it might distract the shaykh from giving them a final blessing. Or, looking at things from an earthlier viewpoint, it might diminish the reputation of the *khanaqah* as well as their ability to gather donations for it in the future. The students also began to talk anxiously among themselves.

Just then, a very loud, high voice out in the street cut through all the hubbub.

"Halvah! Nice sweet halvah! Who wants to buy some? Best halvah in Baghdad!"

Because the voice startled everyone, they all stopped talking for just an instant, but then at once went back to their angst-ridden conversations.

The shaykh motioned to his closest student.

"Ask the boy to come in, let's have some halvah," he rasped.

The student went out into the street and brought the small boy in, who was carrying a large silver plate covered with many pieces of halvah.

"Boy, how much for your whole plate of halvah?" asked the shaykh.

"This is my last plate of halvah for the day, and it's the best halvah in Baghdad. There isn't any even close to this quality in the whole world!" The boy had clearly been well trained. "So, one silver dirham."

"One silver dirham!" exclaimed the shaykh softly, raising one eyebrow in disbelief. "Is the halvah made of silver? No, boy, we're just poor Sufis here. And I'm dying. I'll give you half a silver dirham."

The boy paused, but only for effect, since he knew that the plate was worth only a half of that, and he would need to bring his master back even less.

"All right. But only this once. Because you're dying. And because you're holy people. Or so they say."

"Share it all around," the shaykh told the boy, whispering hoarsely as loudly as he could so that everyone heard. "These are all my brothers and friends here. Let them enjoy the sweetness, just as I am about to enjoy the sweetness of heaven . . . *inshallah* (Allah willing)!"

The boy went around the room, offering halvah to everyone, and by some chance (or indeed miracle), there was enough for all. For some blessed moments, conversation stopped, with only the sound of chewing and smacking of lips breaking the silence. Someone burped.

After a discreet pause, the boy approached the shaykh for payment, holding his hand out.

"Money? You want money? Boy, as I told you, we're only poor Sufis here. I agreed to a price, but I didn't say I would pay you."

The boy became furious.

"You Sufi dogs! You would steal from a poor boy? What kind of people are you? I will be short when I return to the shop. Don't you know that my master will beat me? In fact, he'll probably kill me! In fact, he'll kill my whole family! In fact . . ."

The boy went on in this vein, becoming louder and louder, increasingly and genuinely hysterical, his voice echoing through the mosque.

The creditors also went into an uproar.

"First he cheats us, now he cheats this poor boy!"

"Call the judge!"

"I'll never offer a friendly loan, not to mention a charitable donation, to a Sufi again!"

The students turned bright red and turned to one another, whispering frantically, unsure what to do.

"That's it. The reputation of our whole order is ruined!"

"We're done for!"

"Doesn't anyone have a half a dirham?"

They began to search through their robes.

While all of this was going on, a messenger in richly braided and brightly colored livery entered the room.

"Hey!" he yelled. "Which of you is the shaykh?" As messengers were trained to have loud voices in those days, everyone stopped for an instant, now aware that someone important had likely sent the messenger.

"He is," said one of the creditors, pointing to the shaykh on his bed.

As it happened, the messenger was also carrying a silver tray, this one covered with a silk cloth. He approached the shaykh.

"Someone hired me ten minutes ago to send you this, express delivery. For some reason, it had to be on a silver tray. I don't know who it was, but we work for an expensive service, you know. Had to be someone rich."

The shaykh, who had been resting with his eyes closed during the melee, opened one eye and asked his nearest student to remove the cloth and see what was there.

Under the cloth were two packets also wrapped in silk, one very large, the other very small. When the student untied the larger packet, it was full of gold dinars, more than he had ever seen. There was doubtless enough to pay off all the shaykh's creditors, plus enough to support the khanaqah for some time.

When he untied the small packet, he found it contained half a silver dirham.

The shaykh instructed his students to repay all the creditors, keep the rest, and give the half dirham to the boy.

Everyone was astonished. The boy grabbed the money and ran off with it before anything else crazy happened. These Sufis!

The creditors wiped their brows and breathed a huge sigh of relief. Then they began to protest to the shaykh that, of course, they knew that he was a righteous man and would make good on his debts, and to please pray for them when he got to the other side—in other words, they began to talk total nonsense.

The students were also relieved. Life would go on without them needing to face disaster, like getting jobs outside the khanaqah.

"Master," asked one murid, "how did this happen? How could anyone know about the halvah? And why did he (or she) wait so long to bail us out?"

"Allah knows!" said the shaykh. "But I'll tell you this: all these creditors don't really need the money. They are all rich men many times over. Their distress was all an act. Also, all of you are perfectly capable of making your own way when I'm gone. You may only need to be a little more . . . ingenious. It was only the boy who had real need. You could hear it in his voice.

"When a real cry from the depths of the heart goes out, then Allah always answers. Try to find more genuine need in yourself. Then you will be on the inner path."

The Hodja's Bargain

Once upon a time, a few hundred years ago, in a small town in Ottoman Turkey, there lived a hodja. If you look up the word *hodja* on the Internet, you will find definitions like "religious teacher" or "scholar of Islam." Really, these days we would call a hodja a public intellectual, the type of person the news broadcasters bring on to comment as an expert on some feature of the economy, politics, or foreign relations. Sometimes they really know more; sometimes they only sound like they know more but when you boil it down, they haven't said anything. In the premodern world, there were few job opportunities for intellectuals, so a hodja had to find work where he or she could.

In this case, our hodja taught young boys to read the Qur'an in the local mosque. As was traditional, he did this by having them repeat each passage after him, over and over, until they had learned the words (and hopefully some of the meaning). While they did this, they would rock forward and back, because it's much easier to memorize something if you move your body rhythmically (or so I'm told).

One day the hodja was teaching Sura Al Baqara, the second and longest chapter in the Qur'an. A long way into the sura, just as he was getting ready to wind up for the day, he came to a verse that goes like this:

> *Those who spend what they have in the cause of Allah are like a grain of corn that grows seven ears and each ear yields a hundred more grains. And Allah multiplies the increase to whomever Allah wills.*

The hodja asked one of the youngest boys to repeat the verse for him, and he did so successfully. The hodja breathed a satisfied sigh, then stopped short.

For some reason, perhaps because he was tired, perhaps because a songbird tweeted in the distance in the same key that the boy intoned the passage, perhaps only because this is a story, our hodja was struck by the meaning of the passage, as if he had heard it for the first time.

Does this mean, he thought to himself, *that if I give away everything I have in the name of Allah, I will receive back . . . let's see . . . at least 700 times that amount?*

The hodja looked at the verse again. This seemed to be the plain meaning. In fact, how could it mean anything else?

"Class dismissed!" he called out.

The boys scattered, and the hodja returned home.

He at once gathered all his liquid assets, which was almost everything he owned, since he lived modestly. He calculated. If he received seven hundred times this amount back, he would have a thousand gold dinars. An absolute fortune! He took the money and returned to the mosque, where he gave everything to the imam for the poor. Normally, the rules of *zakat* or charity require that only 2.5 percent of one's income for the year to go to the poor. The imam tried to talk the hodja out of giving so much. Didn't he want to save some for next year? But the hodja was insistent.

He returned home very satisfied and peered into the cupboard for something to eat for supper. What he found was: a half loaf of bread, some olives, and a bit of olive oil. *A little goat cheese might be nice,* he thought. But then he remembered that he had nothing with which to buy it. *Oh well . . . tomorrow I will be repaid.* He sat down to dinner, and the bread, olives, and oil never tasted so good!

When the next day rolled around, the hodja went through the town with a spring in his step. Around every corner he expected to meet a mysterious stranger who would offer him (in Allah's name, of course), a thousand gold dinars. But by the time of his Qur'an class with the boys, there had been no such encounter. The boys noticed that their teacher seemed a bit distracted and kept looking toward the door of the mosque as though he expected someone to walk through any moment.

At the end of the class, the hodja went home and found that only a bit more bread, a few olives, and the remnants of the olive oil were left for supper. He used the rest of the bread to clean the last of the oil out of the jar. He went to bed a bit anxious, but he consoled himself with the thought that Allah was simply testing those whom He loved with the presence of His absence.

The next day, the same scenario occurred (but you probably already guessed that would happen). At the end of the day, the hodja trudged home to the last two olives and a few crumbs of bread that had fallen into the cracks of his table the day before. As he lay in bed, he told himself he still hoped for the best tomorrow. *Inshallah!* But he really expected the worst.

When he awoke the next day, he decided that he needed to be more proactive. Allah was undoubtedly very busy and simply needed reminding. After all, can you imagine all the prayers the Holy One had coming in every moment from all over the world! And many of them contradicting one other (considering the multiplicity of religions).

He could, of course, remind Allah inwardly in prayer, but that somehow seemed too insubstantial. He needed to make a formal petition aloud, much as one would appear before the Sultan and ask courteously for redress of a grievance. Of course, Allah was everywhere, or anywhere, but the hodja didn't want his neighbors to overhear him seeming to complain to Allah. That wouldn't do for his reputation as a hodja.

He decided to go outside the town walls to make his petition, but every time he stopped, someone appeared from behind a tree or around a bend in the road. He kept walking and finally found himself a great distance away from the town near an isolated grove of palm trees. *Finally*, he thought, *just the place!*

Just as he was preparing himself, however, he heard an inhuman howling not too far away. The hodja froze.

He had heard that there was a crazy dervish living in the wilderness around the town accosting people. Accosting might be too mild a word. This dervish was actually very mad, and without consulting a psychological diagnostic manual for specifics, I can tell you that he was aggressive and probably psychopathic. He had been known to attack anyone who didn't give him some donation or whose looks he simply didn't like.

The howling was coming closer and closer. The hodja's mind went into overdrive, as one might count the seconds between a thunderclap and lightning. That's why he was a scholar, after all. At the rate that the howling was approaching, and the distance that he was from the town, the hodja estimated that he would be unable to reach safety before the dervish caught him. Sometimes knowing more just adds to one's despair!

The hodja looked around and found the tallest palm tree. He climbed to the top and hid himself in the branches, just as the dervish appeared from behind a small rise, howling ever more loudly. As luck would have it, the dervish sat down under the same tree in which the hodja was hiding.

The mad dervish seemed to be in some sort of frenzy, shaking his long, matted hair, muttering to himself and rummaging loudly in the small shoulder bag he carried. The hodja peered out from behind some branches and tried to hear what he was saying. The dervish let out a bloodcurdling shout.

"That's it! I've had enough! No one can help you now," he said. He pulled a large curved knife out of his bag and began sharpening it on a whetstone he found in the bag.

The hodja's teeth chattered as he heard the sound, imagining the knife sinking into his flesh.

But the dervish had something else in his fevered brain. He took what appeared to be a small amulet from his bag and began to speak to it.

"You, prophet Job! They say you were the most patient man alive. Yet when God tested you, you cursed God. Even worse, you made people believe there was a reward in the afterlife if they suffered patiently here. Rubbish! For these sins, no one has punished you. I will punish you!"

Placing the amulet on the earth, he stabbed it with the knife, breaking it into many pieces.

Next, he took another amulet out of the bag and looked at it with even more contempt.

"Hey, you! King David! You sang beautiful songs that encouraged people to lead righteous lives. But you slept with someone else's wife and killed her husband. So there was one standard for you and one for everyone else. For misleading everyone and abusing your power, no one has punished you. So now I will punish you—by taking off your head!" The dervish raised the knife and smashed the second amulet.

The procedure was repeated with an amulet representing King Solomon.

"You, Solomon, you were even more wealthy, had all of the advantages and even could speak to the *jinn* [the ones we call genies] and command them to do whatever you wanted with your magic ring. Yet you did many foolish things. In the end, your kingdom collapsed, people suffered, and you brought more misery into the world. No one has yet punished you, so I'll do it!" The amulet flew apart, one piece almost hitting the petrified hodja in the branch above.

Next came Jesus, who despite his humble background, did not escape the hodja's insane anger.

"Hmph . . . Jesus. They call you 'breath of Allah.' You preached peace and lived a righteous life. But after you, those who followed you created all sorts of chaos and suffering, all in your name. Couldn't you have prevented it, if you really were the 'son of God'? You were a great prophet, okay, but the misery you eventually caused must be punished. No one has done it, so it's up to me!" The dervish plunged the knife into the Jesus amulet and twisted it with glee.

You can already see a trend here, I'm sure. It should serve as a testament to the dervish's actual clinical madness that the next amulet he pulled from his bag held an image of the Prophet Muhammad. Images of the Prophet are forbidden, as I'm sure you know, since one should not confuse any human being (or any human being's mistakes) with the Reality behind the cosmos, which is beyond any scripture or religion.

"All right. Prophet Muhammad. Let's look at this objectively," said the dervish, shaking his head in a less-than-objective frenzy, his eyes wild.

"I have killed Job, David, Solomon, and Jesus. What shall I do with you? Yes, you brought a message of unity, saying you made no distinction between any of the prophets. But the rivers ran red with blood, first with that of your own followers fighting each other and then with the devotees of other faiths. What kind of 'unity' is that? No one has punished you, so reluctantly, I have to do it!" The dervish stabbed the amulet repeatedly, until all the pieces had disappeared into soil.

Enough is enough, you might think. But no! There was one more.

The dervish, with still some vestigial remembrance of sanity, prostrated himself on the earth and then took one more amulet out of his bag.

"O Allah! I have punished Job, David, Solomon, Jesus, and Muhammad. But you sent these men, giving them visions or whatever, inspiring them to do whatever they did. And look where we are! What can I say? Meaning no disrespect, but how can I punish them and not you? You have to go, too!" Raising his knife, the dervish inhaled a great gulp of air and prepared to destroy the image of Allah (whatever that might have been).

"Wait!" yelled out the hodja above him. "You can't do that! Allah still owes me a thousand gold dinars!"

The dervish swayed, his eyes rolled up, and he collapsed onto the ground. Appalled at what he had done without thinking, the hodja was petrified and thought his last hour had come. He stayed motionless, watching the form below him. The dervish didn't move.

After a half hour, the dervish still had not moved.

The hodja broke off a small piece of branch from the palm tree and threw it at the dervish. He still didn't move. Next, he threw one of his shoes down at him. Nothing. Finally he climbed down and put his ear to the dervish's heart. He was dead, all right.

The hodja did not feel any compunction about the death. After all, the dervish was mad and was committing sacrilege. He had been a danger to everyone for a while. *At least I won't starve tonight*, thought the hodja. *I'll sell his clothes and bag and buy some bread.*

As he removed the dervish's belt, he found it to be quite heavy. Opening it, he found that it was full of gold. Counting the money, the hodja found that it was exactly one thousand gold dinars.

"Well, Allah," said the hodja, looking up in exasperation. "You finally kept your promise. But I had to save your life before you did!

II

Mullah Nasruddin: International Man of Mysticism

Stories of the wise fool Mullah Nasruddin (sometimes called Hodja Nasruddin) have proliferated all along the Silk Road from the Middle East to China. The city of Bukhara in present-day Uzbekistan claims to be his birthplace. In the center of the old city, you can find a statue of the young, slim, handsome Mullah riding his donkey. This is quite different from the more middle-aged, roly-poly Mullah one sees in Turkish books.

Turkey, of course, also claims to be Nasruddin's home, and one can find another monument, his reputed gravesite, near Konya. It has a locked gate at the entrance but no fence surrounding it.

You can find collections of Mullah's adventures in many different languages and countries throughout the

East, each culture claiming him. Many Mullah stories also appear in other forms in other traditions, for instance, Jewish Hasidism, and it is difficult to tell which came first. No doubt, it doesn't really matter.

Some Mullah stories are little more than one-liners and others very long. As I wrote in *The Sufi Book of Life*, Mullah can stand for various things in various stories. There is no one key to all of them, nor need there be any key at all. We are not in the territory of simple analogy or allegory.

One could say that the whole complex of a Mullah story mirrors back to us deep tendencies of our mind or behavior that we may not have known we had. These impressions, or "voices," lie buried in our *nafs* (similar to the subconscious). So when we recognize ourselves in a story, the laughter disarms and hopefully illuminates a part of our inner self. The story points indirectly to a way for our "inner jungle" of animals to find their purpose in the greater whole of our soul's purpose (see the last selection in this book). But perhaps that type of language is much too sublime for someone like Mullah!

The first group of stories comes from Mullah's home in Uzbekistan. They are followed by a sample of the many stories about Mullah and his donkey. There are many more in my earlier book.

The second group gathers together my favorites in the genre of "Mullah as public official," very pertinent for today, I think. Gradually, Mullah begins to climb the ladder of government. Even then, the way into politics often began with the law. These types of Nasruddin stories border on social satire, so storytellers often adapt them to fit local conditions and events.

The next two stories unfold a bit more slowly and take us back to the theme of Mullah and animal husbandry. Concluding the group is a short one that shows Mullah in a "Zen" frame of mind.

Uzbek Stories of Mullah

WHERE DO WE GO?

When Nasruddin was a young boy, he was walking with his father through their village. They saw a funeral procession pass by, the men carrying the coffin and chanting "There is no reality but Reality." In respect, his father stopped and offered a prayer while the cortege passed. Taking the opportunity, he then tried to educate his son about death, where the soul goes, and "the other side."

"All right," said young Nasruddin, "but I still don't understand. If what you call the soul continues and is now free, where are they taking that thing in the box?"

His father decided to use a metaphor rather than shock the boy.

"They are taking him to a place where there is very little space, no windows, no cozy family hearth, and no food. Understand?"

"Yes, I've got it!" said the boy. "They are taking him to our house!"

PROFESSIONAL EXPERT

Due to his quick mind, Nasruddin tried for a while to make his living by offering expert advice to others. People came to him under the assumption that, as a hodja, he had better access to the unseen than other people did.

Once a very pious man came trying to trick him.

"You, hodja, are nearly a saint," said the man. "You can hear the voice of Allah more clearly than we other mere mortals are able to. Can you tell me: what is a thousand years in the sight of Allah?"

Nasruddin gazed into the sky for a moment before he responded.

"One second."

"And what," asked the man, "is the value of a thousand gold bars for the Almighty?"

Mullah didn't hesitate.

"One little copper coin."

"So, can you, O Sage of Sages, ask Allah to give me this particular small copper coin?"

Nasruddin gazed into the sky again and replied.

"Allah says: of course. Just wait a second."

DUELING EXPERTS

Once a traveling wise man came to town and challenged Mullah to a dual of hodjas. When people heard about it, they came to the village square and crowded around the two men.

"I accept your challenge," said Mullah. "It's my turf, so here is the test. If you ask me forty different questions, I will give one answer to them all. If I can, you lose." The traveler agreed and asked forty very complex questions.

Mullah responded, "I don't know anything."

Everyone groaned but agreed that the home team had won.

POINT OF VIEW

Once another challenger asked Mullah to prove his special powers as a hodja and favored one of Allah.

"I can see in the dark," replied Mullah placidly.

"Why then," asked his challenger, "do I see you wandering around the streets at night with a lighted candle in your hand?"

"Easy. That's so people who can't see in the dark don't bump into me and hurt themselves."

BALANCING ACT

One day during a rainstorm Mullah was walking along the street. He slipped and was about to fall into a puddle when a man grabbed his arm and pulled him upright.

"A million thanks, my friend," said Mullah. "I might have fallen and I have only one good cloak, this being it."

"Don't mention it," replied the man, with some self-satisfaction. "As a wise man, I'm sure you know: people should help one another."

Thereafter, whenever Mullah saw the man in town, the man waved and said to him effusively, "Remember, people should help one another!" Mullah thanked him again and moved on. This happened over and over.

As it so happened, one day it rained again. Mullah saw the man walking along the street toward him. Before the man could say a word, Mullah took his arm and dragged him to the same puddle on the same street as before. Then Mullah flopped into the puddle.

"Look!" said Nasruddin, "Now I'm wet because of you! Now you are in my debt. Better stay away from me!"

The man, however, had already disappeared.

Donkeys

SOME CONSOLATION

Mullah was often losing his donkey. Once while he was looking for it, he was walking through town, singing and giving thanks to God.

"Why are you so joyful, Mullah?" his friends asked him. "We thought you had *lost* your favorite donkey."

"I did, friends," responded Mullah. "But at least I wasn't riding it at the time. If I had been, I would be lost, too!"

A BARGAIN IS A BARGAIN

Once when Mullah lost his donkey, he decided to go to the local Sufi shrine, the burial place of a saint. He pledged that if he found the donkey, he would donate ten gold dinars to the restoration of the saint's shrine.

Shortly thereafter, he found the donkey.

Mullah returned to the shrine and spoke to the dead saint.

"It seems that you are a man of your word. How about this? I will give the ten gold dinars for your shrine plus another ten if you allow me to find a hundred gold dinars without working for them!"

DEFECTIVE GOODS?

By dint of poverty, Mullah finally had to sell his favorite donkey.

However, shortly after he sold it the donkey died. The new owner complained.

"I don't know what to tell you," said Mullah. "It never did that with me!"

Mullah in Civil Service

LEGAL TRAINING

Mullah decided that being a local expert and depending on donations was too precarious a living. And donkeys, well, they seemed to have a mind of their own! He decided to train in the law, as someone told him that this was the way to success. Talk a lot, use logic, and make money for doing not much else.

Since he had no money for legal training, he agreed to apprentice with a legal expert informally. Nasruddin promised to pay him from the proceeds of the first case he won. He signed a contract to that effect.

However, Mullah lost interest as soon as he completed his training and never worked as a lawyer. Naturally, his mentor brought him to court for nonpayment of the debt.

Mullah presented his case to the judge.

"Your Honor, if I win this case, then by definition the esteemed plaintiff, my former mentor, will not be paid, because I will have refuted his claim.

"However, if I should lose the case, then I also will not have to pay him, since by the terms of the contract we signed, I would not yet have won a case."

"Case dismissed," said the judge, scratching his head.

STANDARDS OF SERVICE

After he won his case against his former mentor, the news of Mullah's facility with the law spread. Without having to work as a lawyer, he was appointed as a local judge for his town.

One day as he was presiding over the small-claims court, a man rushed in wearing only his shirt. No trousers, shoes, or hat—only his shirt and one didn't even know if there was anything under that.

"Help! I've been robbed!" cried the man. "I demand justice and compensation!"

"All right," said Mullah in a bored tone of voice that he had heard other judges use. "Describe the case to me fully."

"It's simple. I am a foreigner and a visitor to your town. I came to sell my goods in the market. As I was entering the gates early this morning, I was set upon by thieves who stole everything—my donkey, my goods, all my clothes even! What kind of town is this that can't guarantee the safety of a poor visiting merchant? I demand some compensation from the court!"

Mullah sighed. The man no doubt had a case, and the town didn't want to get a bad reputation for commerce.

However, Mullah was under instructions from above to conserve expenses at all costs.

"I see," said Mullah, "that they *did* leave you your shirt."

"Yes, thank God! If they had taken that I would be completely naked!"

"My friend," said Mullah, "I'm sorry. It can't have been anyone from our town. We have a strict law on the books that any job begun must be finished completely. Even our thieves obey this. Next case!"

QUALITY CONTROL

In the local bureaucracy, Mullah gradually gained a reputation for wise (and economical) decisions. Naturally, he was given a promotion. Instead of presiding over minor cases all day, he was delegated to inspect the quality of goods and customer service in the market. This was known to be a plum job, since the merchants usually offered a lot of freebies and perks to get on the good side of the market inspector.

All was going well when one day a magician came into the center of the market and parked his wagon there. Many people started to flock around. A magician was always entertaining, and everyone wanted to believe in magic.

"Gather round, gather round!" called out the magician. "I can not only show you the usual tricks, but I really am in control of unseen forces! I can prove it!"

Mullah thought this claim went too far. Being a master trickster is one thing, but claiming power over the unseen couldn't be correct and violated the town's ordinance about truth in advertising. He strode through the crowd and confronted the magician.

"All right, all right. What's this you say about unseen forces? I am the official market inspector, and I demand to see any proof you have. We demand truth in advertising here; otherwise I'll have to ask you leave town."

"Easy, easy, don't worry, my friend," said the magician. "Tell me, are you able to read?"

Mullah was a bit embarrassed but had to admit that he didn't. He had come this far by his common sense, and anyway, why did he need to read?

"Okay," said the magician, and placing his hand on Mullah's forehead, he mumbled some foreign-sounding magic words. "There!" he said after a few seconds. "You can now read!"

"How will I know?" asked Mullah.

"Well, go find a book!"

Mullah left the market and went back to courthouse where he used to work.

"Do we have any books here?" he asked the clerk.

"Yes, there's a whole roomfull in there," the clerk replied, pointing to a room that held the reference library for staff.

Mullah went into the room.

Several hours later, he came running back into the marketplace.

"Where is that magician, that fraud! I'm going to arrest him, then put him in jail! Then after a long time, I'll run him out of town!"

"Mullah, he left an hour ago," said a friend. "He did many wonderful tricks, made a lot of money, and drove off. Why are you so angry? Aren't you able to read as he promised?"

"No, I can read all right, but I just read in an encyclopedia that all magicians are frauds! Now, which way did he go?"

A QUESTION OF THE EMPLOYER

Mullah's diligence did not go unnoticed in high places. His reputation eventually brought him to the attention of the sultan himself, who asked Mullah to serve as one of his advisers in court.

Of course, in those days, such a position could be as precarious as it was beneficial. The process for removal had no appeal and, for the former official, a low survival rate.

One day, the cook prepared for the sultan a particularly tasty eggplant dish, a secret recipe for *baba ghanoush.* The sultan liked it so much that he ordered the cook to put it on the menu every day for lunch.

"Eggplants are the tastiest vegetables in the world!" enthused the sultan.

"Yes, my liege," agreed Nasruddin. "They are undoubtedly the tastiest!"

However, the sultan quickly became tired of the same dish. Five days later, he had changed his tune.

"Take this away! I can't stand the taste anymore," he said.

"I agree, my liege," said Nasruddin. "Eggplants are the least tasty vegetables in the world."

"But only a few days ago," said the sultan, "you agreed that eggplants were the tastiest vegetables in the world. How do you explain that?"

"Easy," said Mullah. "I work for the sultan, not for the eggplants."

THE VALUE OF GOOD SELF-ESTEEM

One day, Mullah walked into court wearing a particularly ostentatious and regal-looking turban. The sultan asked him about it.

"You know, my liege," said Mullah, "this turban cost me a thousand gold dinars."

"That's absurd!" said another courtier. "No turban can be worth that much."

"You're wrong there," replied Mullah. "I paid that much because I knew that only our sultan would have the keen eye and discriminating taste to be able to recognize that a turban like this, of the highest possible quality, was really worth two thousand gold dinars."

The sultan quickly ordered his treasurer to pay Mullah two thousand gold dinars and promptly settled the turban on his own head.

Later Mullah told the other courtier, "Maybe I can't estimate the value of turbans, but I can estimate the value of our sultan's self-esteem."

POSSIBLE PROMOTION

The sultan was always looking for clever officials to promote who knew how to save money and appeared to be doing much for the common people. To him, Mullah seemed to be one of these, and so he invited Nasruddin to an audience to talk about his prospects.

Mullah entered the throne room and bowed to the sultan respectfully.

"O my liege, your humble servant is at your service."

"Mullah," began the sultan, "you've done well in my court. I also heard good things about your work as a judge and market inspector. All your supervisors filed reports to say that you were always busy in a very visible way but at the same time spent a minimum of resources in going about your job. We have several higher positions open that I'd like you to consider.

"There is, for instance, the supervisor of all mullahs. Or the chief accountant, who keeps track of the gifts that my retainers give me. There is even assistant under-vizier—that is, the adviser to the adviser to the closest adviser to me. With a job like that, who knows how far you could go? Or I could give you a whole district to run. What do you say?"

"Do you have anything else, my liege?" asked Mullah. "I want to make an informed decision."

"Very wise," the sultan replied and went on for a half hour describing many different positions and their qualifications. Several of them could eventually prove very lucrative.

"That's it, I think," said the sultan, exhaling loudly. "Well, which will it be?"

"I'm not really interested in any of those," said Mullah. "The one job I'd really like is yours. There doesn't seem to be any qualification, and I would control everyone and have as much wealth as I want."

"My job!" cried the sultan. "What, are you crazy?"

Mullah scratched his chin for a moment.

"Maybe," he said. "Is that the main qualification?"

Mullah and the Camel Seeds

It was with great reluctance that Mullah hastily left his position in civil service. But he had climbed as high as he could go, and after the last audience with the sultan, well, he wasn't given much of a choice.

Mullah headed back to the marketplace. Wistfully, he passed through the donkey dealers section. He had already tried buying and selling donkeys, and he had more or less mastered the occupation. He knew he could always go back to it. However, he was looking for something new, something fresh, something . . . easy and profitable!

As he reached a section of the market between the donkeys and the cows, in a sort of no-animal's-land, he passed by the stall of a young man who was calling out, "Camel seeds! Get your fresh camel seeds here! Easy to grow—easy money here!"

"Hmm," thought Mullah, inspecting a tableful of what appeared to be large, brown clumps with pieces of straw sticking out of them here and there. They all smelled . . . pungent. He thought he knew something about livestock, but he had never heard of camel seeds. Easy money, though, the man had said.

"Young man, I'm interested," he said. "Can you tell me exactly how they work? How do you grow them?"

"Just like any other seed, of course," replied the man. "You take them home, plant them in the ground, and water them. Nothing to it. I guess you aren't very knowledgeable about animals."

"I was mainly in other livestock," said Mullah, embarrassed. "I didn't know you could grow camels from seed."

"Yes, of course!" said the young man. "Many people don't realize it. That's why they grow so tall. And you don't have all the expense of buying new stock, or the stress of delivering baby camels—all that mess."

"I see," said Mullah. "All right, how much for nine of these?"

The young man quoted a price, which seemed high for the strange-smelling clumps, but if each one produced a camel, the profit would be huge. So Mullah gave him what amounted to all the money he had with him, and he headed home with the nine large seeds cradled in his arms. Up close they smelled even more pungent.

When Mullah returned home, he went into the grassy field attached to his house and planted them all, spaced evenly. He watered the seeds faithfully each day and waited for them to grow. While he waited, he began to fence in the field so that when the camels grew, they wouldn't escape. Each day he built another section of fence so that he would feel he was making some progress.

As the days went by, not much seemed to be happening. The areas where he had planted the seeds seemed to be somehow greener, and the grass grew higher, but there was no sign of any camel life.

If it's true that a watched pot never boils, then it must also be true that a watched camel seed doesn't grow, thought Mullah. He decided to take the next day off, go to his old haunt, the local teahouse, and enjoy the company of his friends. He had almost finished the fence and was sure that the seeds were well watered.

The next day Mullah left for the teahouse after breakfast and enjoyed the whole day there, mostly telling stories about his exploits as a civil servant.

A short time before he left, a camel merchant from a village in the neighboring valley brought nine camels into the town, heading for the market, but he decided to stop at the teahouse first. He loosely tied the camels outside and went in. The camels, however, were also in need of refreshment and, under the influence of the most rebellious of them, pulled their leads free and headed off in search of food. Close by, they came upon Mullah's field, with nine large tufts of juicy, green grass. Perfect! They entered the field and were happily munching away when Mullah returned home and saw them.

"Praise God!" he cried. "My camels have grown! Just as I thought—I was watching them too much."

He quickly finished the remaining section of the fence so that the camels couldn't escape, then went into his house satisfied with the whole day's events.

He wasn't home more than an hour when he heard a banging on his door. It was, of course, the camel merchant.

"Hey! Those are my camels! Why do you have them fenced in?"

"Your camels?" replied Mullah. "My friend, I'm afraid you're mistaken. I grew those camels from seed. I started them maybe a month ago, and today they've finally grown up."

"Grew them from seed? Don't be absurd!" said the camel merchant.

An argument ensued. Rather than come to blows, however, both men decided to present their case to a local judge. Mullah had great faith in the judicial system, having been a local judge himself.

When they arrived in court, both men presented their stories. The camel merchant offered his case with great lucidity and logic. He was a visitor to town, he had temporarily parked his camels at a teahouse, and when he came out they had been stolen by this crazy man, who could only offer an impossible story about having grown them from seed.

Mullah knew the local judge, because they had once worked together.

"Your Honor, I purchased camel seeds in the market a month or so ago. And as you know, our merchants only sell honest goods. Then I planted them according to instructions. Today they finally grew into adult camels. Hand on heart, I swear that's exactly what happened." As he said the last sentence, he placed his hand inside his robe over his heart, and moved it up and down.

Now Mullah's gesture was universally understood in the local judiciary to mean only one thing: if you rule in my favor, I'll put my hand in my pocket and make it worth your while. This was not lost on the judge.

"Let me consider for a few moments," he said and sat pretending to make notes on a piece of paper in front of him.

After a suitable pause, he said, "Having considered all the evidence as well as the variables of circumstance, probability, veracity, and *character*," and here he paused for effect, "I find for Mullah Nasruddin. The camels are his."

Disgusted, the camel merchant left town and was never seen there again. The next day, Mullah was at home preparing to go sell his camels when he heard another knock on the door. It was, yes, the judge.

"Mullah," said the judge, "as you know I found in your favor yesterday and you led me to believe that there would be some remuneration involved."

"Remuneration?" said Mullah. "But bribery is strictly outlawed in our town. Oh, you mean my hand-on-heart gesture? That was me saying that I was holding a large rock there, and if you didn't rule in my favor, I would throw it at you. Sorry, but you misunderstood the signals. Better luck next time!"

Mullah Tries Donkeys Again

Although Mullah felt that he had done well with his camel seeds, he decided they were too much trouble if he was going to end up in court each time. There were so many unscrupulous camel merchants about that he didn't want to get into bad company continually. He supposed it had something to do with a camel's often cantankerous character.

"I need to get back to something I know," said Mullah to himself. "Why not try donkeys again?"

Mullah returned to the donkey market, which he knew very well from years ago. Mullah really knew his donkeys. There was everything from your basic, no-frills, working person's donkey to the all-bells-and-whistles, gold-toothed luxury donkey. Or from the nondescript, very average-looking donkey, great for smuggling things, to the barely domesticated, wild racing donkey, suitable for the donkey-racing aficionado. No one could put anything over on Mullah in the donkey area, so he was supremely confident.

When Mullah arrived in the market, he looked over the stock available. The trick was, as always, to buy the best for the lowest price, then go somewhere else and resell it for more. Or perhaps put in a few cosmetic improvements (like a saddlebag or bridle), then resell. In that way, one climbed the proverbial "donkey ladder." Soon he would again be dealing only with the best clients (and he still had a few in his address book).

As Mullah wandered around, he saw nothing very distinguished. All the animals were very average, and there was no price point to take advantage of. In fact, prices for average donkeys seemed to have gone up in the years that he had been out of the business. Maybe he would need to reconsider . . . .

As Mullah was nearing the edge of the market, however, he saw an excellent donkey. Good size, haunches, muzzle. It was a bit dirty, but that was easily remedied. Quality reveals itself. The young owner, looking a bit desperate, was standing all alone, with only the one donkey on a simple rope lead.

"This one I can do something with," thought Mullah. "And one has to start somewhere." He asked the owner how much he wanted. It was an excellent price, less than the very average donkeys were selling for in the rest of the market.

"Well, I don't know," said Mullah to the young man. "How long have you been in business? I only like to buy from reputable people. What if there is a problem?"

"I'm only recently in business, sir," said the young man. "My father died and left me with a small stock of donkeys. I don't really know much about them, but I need to sell them to feed my wife and children, not to mention my ailing mother who also lives with us, all in one room."

Mullah listened, nodding contemplatively. Then, after an appropriate pause, he agreed to buy the donkey and handed over the money.

"Oh, thank you, sir!" said the young man. "You've been so kind. I'm sure that you'll have no trouble with this animal. He was my father's favorite."

A spring in his step, Mullah walked home very happily, the donkey on a lead behind him. On the way, he decided to stop at the teahouse to celebrate. A small beginning, but very promising. A good omen. He tied the donkey outside and went in. When he came out about an hour later, instead of the donkey tied at the rail, he saw a strange young man with the donkey's lead tied around his neck, looking hopeful.

"Who are you? What are you doing here?" asked Mullah. "And where is my donkey?"

"Oh sir!" said the young man effusively. "I'm so grateful to you! Long ago, an evil magician enchanted me and turned me into a donkey. For years, I've wandered about working for a few oats and sleeping on a simple bed of straw—a hard life! Can you imagine what that was like? The only thing that could free me was for a saint to buy me. Hurrah! That's you! Thank you so much!"

"But I bought a donkey," grumbled Mullah. "What am I supposed to do with you? You're a human being, so no good to ride on."

The young man looked at him expectantly with large, innocent eyes.

"Oh, all right, you! Get along! You're free. Just remember to tell people which saint freed you."

The young man ran off into the town, and Mullah headed home muttering to himself. Now this was something he hadn't encountered before. The donkey business had become much more complicated.

Nonetheless, the next day, he decided to try again. He went through the market, this time more slowly. Nothing. Nothing. And more nothing. Then in the same location, he again saw what was surely the same donkey he had bought yesterday, only this time being sold by a different young man.

Mullah walked over brimming with righteous indignation. Going up to the donkey, he put his face right in the animal's muzzle and declared,

"Confess! You're a human being! You fooled me once, for sure. But you certainly won't fool me a second time!"

Not Myself: The Zen Mullah

Mullah decided to travel for a while, and during this time, he obtained renown as a visiting Sufi.

Once he was staying overnight in a Sufi *khanaqah*. As was usual, this one had an open hall where traveling dervishes could stay for up to three nights, a bit like a Sufi hostel. As it so happened, someone at his last stop had given Mullah a large, very tasty pita bread sandwich.

Mullah was sitting on a bench eating it when one of the other dervishes sidled up to him and began to look longingly at the sandwich.

"You know, Nasruddin, I've heard of you. You're a famous Sufi."

Mullah mumbled something unintelligible and continued eating the sandwich.

"I learned from my esteemed shaykh," said the dervish, "that the proper *adab* or manner among dervishes is to prefer our brother's welfare to our own. Me, I'm now so free inside that I can only think of others, and not of myself at all." He paused for effect, still staring at the sandwich. "What do you think, Mullah?"

Mullah finished chewing the mouthful he was on and then looked at the dervish.

"That's very good, brother. *Mashallah!* May Allah make it so. There is still some way to go, however. Take me. I've become so objective and detached that I can only think of myself *as* another person. That's how I can endure thinking first of the welfare of this other person, me."

And he continued finishing the sandwich.

III

Stories about Jesus

The Islamic and Sufi traditions tell many stories about Jesus, whom the Qur'an calls *Issa* or *Ruh Allah*. Of course, in Aramaic, his name was something like Yeshua (from "Yah," the Living One, and "shua," saves or redeems). It was a common name in the Middle East at the time, and we find variants in the Hebrew biblical names usually spelled in English bibles Joshua and Jehoshua.

The Qur'an calls Jesus *Ruh Allah* ("breath of the One"), because in Sura Maryam, dedicated to Jesus' mother, Issa is born from the breath of God (Joseph is not mentioned). Because of this, he can transmit the "breath of life" to others and so raise people from the dead. The Qur'an, for instance, references a story like one related by one of the Thomas gospels about Jesus as a boy giving life to clay birds.

Undoubtedly, the type of Christianity with which the Prophet Muhammad had contact in 7th-century Arabia had similarities to the Thomas "Jesus movement." It did not feature the notion of the Trinity that had won the theological wars in the late Roman Empire and so did not take part in the Western creeds (like the Nicene Creed). In addition, this Aramaic-Arabic-speaking Christianity held what historians call a "low Christology"—that is, it viewed Jesus as a "son" (small *s*) of God, meaning that there is one God/Reality, and we can all fulfill our purpose as "children of God."

In some Sufi stories, Jesus raises various people or animals from the dead (not just Lazarus, as in the Gospels). This sometimes leads to unexpected consequences and the opportunity for some learning. It's best to see these Sufi Jesus stories as teaching stories rather than as an attempt to relate an alternative history to the Gospels. The "Issa" part of us often points our connection to our guidance or intuition, and how we learn to handle this alternative "way of knowing" in relation to being human.

You can find variations on our first story in the Syriac Eastern Christian stories of Jesus. The version here is from one of the Islamic "tales of the prophets" collections, with my own improvisation.

The second story also comes from a traditional folk collection circulated in the Islamic world from the 13th-century CE onward.

The next two short stories are from early Islamic collections of Jesus' *hadith* or sacred sayings. Sufis retold these over the centuries in part to criticize the luxurious lifestyle and corrupt behavior of Islamic rulers, who ignored the plight of the poor and lived so differently from prophets like Jesus and Muhammad.

The last story is again from Jelaluddin Rumi's *Mathnawi*. It unfolds there in several episodes, interspersed by other stories and commentary.

Young Jesus Goes to School

When Issa was a young boy in Egypt, maybe about five, his mother Maryam thought that he should go to school. This was really nothing for him to learn, since he already seemed to know everything. However, Maryam felt that young Issa needed the presence of other children and to learn a bit of discipline. It didn't quite turn out that way.

The first day Issa went to school, the other children were learning their ABGs (Aramaic, you understand . . . *aleph, beth, gimmel* . . .). The teacher would point to each letter and ask the children to name a word, any simple word, that began with that letter. Each of the children struggled through a letter or two with some prompting. Then, to be kind, the teacher moved on to the next student. Finally, he came to Issa.

"Now, here's our new pupil. Do you know any words from the ABGs, young Issa?"

Issa started at the beginning:

"A is for *aleph*, which stands for *Alaha*, the One Being behind the universe.

"B is for *beth*, which stands for *Bereshith*, the Hebrew word for 'in the beginning,' that begins our creation story, but which really means 'in wings, in flame, from an unknowable otherness.'

"G is for *gimmel*, which stands for either *gan eden*, the Garden of Bliss, in which Adam and Eve first found themselves, or for *gematria*, the science of numerology in the alphabet by which one divines hidden meaning from sacred words . . . ."

Issa went on like this through the whole alphabet. The teacher, unfortunately, was so shocked that he had a heart attack and died.

"Anything unusual happen today at school?" Maryam asked her son when he returned home.

"Not really, Mother, except that the teacher died unexpectedly."

"How strange!"

Now Maryam would have thought no more about it, except that the next day when Issa returned from school she asked him the same question. And received the same answer.

"Now, Issa! Tell me exactly what's been going on at school. What did the teacher do, and what did you do? I want it all."

Issa told her.

"I thought it must be something like this," said Maryam. "Issa, I want you to raise both of those poor teachers from the dead again. You must learn to take responsibility and not to make such a show of yourself. It's part of the training of your human self."

So Issa raised both teachers from the dead and began to learn about being different: sometimes being as wise as a snake, sometimes being as innocent and straightforward as a dove.

Jesus in the Graveyard

Once Issa was passing through a graveyard and met a young man sitting next to a freshly dug mound of dirt. The man was weeping bitterly.

"Who was it?" asked Issa, patting him on the shoulder.

"O Ruh Allah! My beloved wife. We had been together only a few months when she was taken from me. Couldn't you bring her back to me?"

Taking pity on the young man, Issa breathed the breath of life toward the mound, and in an instant, the young woman was standing next to the grave, looking around her, somewhat bewildered.

"O my beloved!" exclaimed the young man. "This is Issa, and he has raised you from the dead. Look, we have another chance to be together!"

The young woman smiled sweetly but was still a bit dazed. The two went off together and sat for a while in a nearby garden to let things sink in.

Issa continued on his way.

As the afternoon became warmer, the young man put his head in his wife's lap and dozed off.

However, it just so happened that a half hour later, a rich and handsome young prince rode by on his horse and, seeing the young woman, gave her "the eye." She gave him "the eye" back. No sooner than you could say *nesyuna* (forgetfulness in Aramaic), the young woman lifted her husband's head gently from her lap and laid it on the grass, allowing him to sleep on. Then she hopped onto the horse with the young prince, and they rode off together.

When the young man awoke, he thought he had dreamed Issa raising his wife from the dead, but he was convinced she was alive. He began to ask all he met if they had seen her. Eventually someone pointed him to the prince's palace. There he found the two of them sitting in the palace garden in a loving embrace. He confronted them, of course.

"Hey, that's my wife!" cried the young man.

"Wife? Wife? Are you his wife?" the prince asked the young woman innocently.

"No, no, never saw him before," she replied.

Now it just so happened that Issa was passing by on his way home and saw the three of them together.

"Issa!" cried the young man, "We need your help!"

"Yes?"

"This prince has stolen my wife, and now she denies knowing me."

"Who is this?" said the prince, pointing to Issa. "And what does he have to do with us?"

"This is Issa, the Breath of God, and he raised my wife from the dead just a few hours ago," said the young man.

"Is that true?" the prince asked the young woman.

"No, no, never saw him before," she replied nonchalantly.

"Then," said Issa to her, "I'm afraid you have to give back the gift I gave you." He inhaled and the young woman disappeared, returning to the grave.

Issa walked away, scratching his head.

"I see now that a second chance is not always better," he said to himself. "I need to be more careful and ask Alaha if it's really mine to do before I change the course of someone's destiny."

Wandering Dervish

THE WORLD IS A BRIDGE

Many Sufi stories of Jesus feature him as a wandering dervish, traveling continually without any home or possessions.

In one story, some followers catch up with him and offer to build him a small house so that he will have a place to teach as well as rest.

Issa agrees and tells them that he knows the perfect place. They follow him as he leads them further into the wild, jungle-like territory that is often mistranslated as "desert" in the Gospels.

Issa leads them to the edge of a river that was flowing rapidly with the spring runoff from Mt. Hermon. He pointed to the middle of the river.

"Just there, my friends. Build my house there!"

"But Ruh Allah, breath of the eternal! How can we build your house in the middle of a river?

"Just so, friends. How can you expect to capture the breath of the One within a structure made by human hands? Haven't you heard the saying, 'The world is a bridge, walk on it, cross over it, but don't build your house on it?'"

STONE FOR A PILLOW

Another time, Issa was traveling by himself, with only a stone under his arm that he used for a pillow.

A tempting spirit interrupted his thoughts.

In the Islamic tradition, this is *Iblis*, about whom I will tell you more later. In the Aramaic Christian Gospels, this spirit is called either *akel karsha* (literally, "self-preoccupation") or *satana* ("what leads astray"). Neither are proper names in Aramaic (which like Hebrew has no capital letters—go ahead and cross them all out in your Bible).

At the time of Jesus, the late Hebrew tradition did not have a notion of a "devil" as an "anti-God"—that is, an entity separate from the all-embracing and unnamable divine Unity itself. These spirits were like obsessive tendencies of mind that could lead one astray from remembering Reality. We might find the same tendencies around or within us today. Was the demon "outside" or "inside"? Again, Hebrew and Aramaic blur the distinction, since the same preposition that means "within" also can mean "among."

Back to our story . . . .

"Ah," said the spirit. "I see that, although you pride yourself on traveling without possessions, you still keep that stone for a pillow, Issa. Hah!"

"Hah, yourself!" replied Issa and threw the stone at the spirit.

This story becomes the origin of the ritual of throwing a stone at a pillar, which occurs in the middle of the annual ritual pilgrimage (*hajj*) in Islam. The fact that this has become one of the most dangerous parts of the pilgrimage gives one pause for thought.

THE TEETH OF THE DOG

Once Issa and his students were walking along a path in Galilee. As they came around a bend, one of the disciples saw on one side of the path ahead of them a dead dog, surrounded by a host of flies.

He nudged one of the other disciples, and the two of them began to gently herd the whole group, together with Jesus, to the other side of the path, shielding the master from the sight. Dead animals of any sort were unclean and dead dogs in particular.

Issa, however, also saw the dead dog and headed straight for it.

Finally, followed by his appalled students, he was standing right in front of the corpse, staring down at it. The animal had been dead some days. The smell was fierce, and there were really many flies.

"Shall we move on, Master?" said one of the disciples tactfully, after a minute or two.

"Not quite yet," replied Issa. "Haven't you noticed how bright is the light coming from its gleaming teeth?"

JESUS AND THE FOOL

One day, a friend of Issa was traveling in the wilderness north of the Sea of Galilee, which as I mentioned was like a jungle wetland at the time. It was not drained for agriculture until the 20th century.

In those days, all sorts of animals and birds inhabited the area. If you visit what remains of the Hula Valley wetland area in Israel, you will find a small museum that documents how many different species, including big cats, lived there.

Digression over.

Issa's friend saw him running through the fields of reeds, jumping over ponds, up and down small hills. He thought nothing of it, but later in the day, as he continued on his way, Issa ran by him again, and the man called out to him.

"Peace be to you, O Issa Ruh Allah!"

As was proper, Issa stopped and replied, "Peace to you, my friend. Good to see you!"

"O Issa Ruh Allah, I saw you running earlier. And now, many hours later, I find you still running. Why?"

"O my friend, I am trying to escape a fool. He is constantly following me, and when he catches up with me, he is always asking very foolish questions.

"You understand," he continued, "I don't mind educating people if they are really in need of knowledge or wisdom. But this fool asks only questions that are totally irrelevant to both his practical and spiritual life. I have tried to tell him this, but the more I tell him, or try to put him on the straight path, the more foolish questions he comes up with. All sorts of things about the metaphysics of this life or the hereafter, about this technique or that spiritual practice. I tried giving him prayers and practices, but he doesn't even try them. Only more questions!"

"Yes, Ruh Allah," replied his friend. "I'm sure that is aggravating. But with all due respect, don't you know the secret name of God? Couldn't you try that on him?"

"Tried it. Nothing happened."

"But what about the 'breath of Allah' that you carry. You have made clay birds fly and raised all sorts of people from the dead, or so I've heard. Couldn't you breathe that breath into him? That should do something."

"Same. No effect."

"But why, O Ruh Allah?"

"Allah knows, but as far as I can tell, his foolishness is not from genuine, honest ignorance. For that there is always a solution. Nor is it from lack of life experience. His foolishness stems from sheer perversity. He lives in a self-involved bubble created by his own concepts, instead of seeing the life actually in front of him. If you can't see and be amazed by Sacred Unity somewhere—in another person, your community, nature, or work—then it's likely you won't find unity or satisfaction anywhere. So his foolishness is already a punishment from Allah, because he treats his own ego as if it were the Only Being."

"Yes, you're probably right, Ruh Allah. Then I'd better let you get on your way before he catches up with you. *Eth-phatah* (May your way be open) and peace to you!"

Issa ran off. And he continued running or perhaps jogging, since the terrain was very uneven. But eventually even he ran out of puff (well, just a bit) and had to stop for a rest. He *was* part human, after all, even excluding his breath.

As he sat under a tree, it just so happened that out of the brush came the fool who had been following him. Obviously, in addition to being a fool, he was part bloodhound. Jesus groaned a bit inside.

"O Issa, Ruh Allah! I'm so glad I've found you! Now, yes, I know I've been bothering you just a bit with my questions . . . ."

"Yes, true," said Issa.

"But . . . but . . . as I was following you, I passed by a certain place, and I just know that if I take you there and I ask you something, all of my questions will be answered! I won't have any more questions, and I won't bother you ever again. I promise! Really, this is a deep intuition or guidance that has come to me, and by the way, I found out recently that I'm psychic, so this just manifests the dream that the soothsayer interpreted for me last week in which I was taken up to the sixth plane of angels and conversed there with all of the other holy psychic people, who welcomed me and gave me a huge banquet, which I can describe in detail for you, if you'd like, and . . . ."

"Just a moment, my friend!" interrupted Issa. "Allow me to commune with the Holy One about this."

Now, Issa was genuinely tempted. If this would really be the end of the fool's questions and him following Issa . . . well, then! However, because he had personal preferences, he felt even more that he should pray to the One for guidance. And pray hard, and quickly, in case the fool's mind wandered onto some other topic again! So, he relaxed and breathed, and breathed more deeply. In his own breath, he felt the "yes" of the Holy One, and he knew he had to follow that. I mean, if you were Ruh Allah and couldn't trust your breath, what kind of sense would that make?

"All right, my friend. Take me where we need to go."

The two traveled for a long distance through the wetlands. They passed by flocks of large cranes nesting and saw a wild dog dart under a bush. A type of water buffalo lifted its head and snorted at them as they walked by. Finally, the fool stopped in front of a small mound of earth that had some bones sticking out of it.

"Here it is, O Ruh Allah!"

"Here what is, my friend?"

"This pile of bones! I have the very firm impression—and I now know that I'm psychic—that if you only raise this pile of bones from the dead, all will be perfect. I know you can, because you've done similar things many times already, all over the place. So why not here? All my questions will be answered. I know it. There won't be any more. Will you do it? Will you? Will you?"

This was now a little more than Issa had in mind. Following the fool so that he could ask him "one more question" was one thing. Raising an unknown pile of bones was another. He had previously had some unexpected surprises when he had raised bones, thinking he would be helping people.

Again Issa returned in prayer and meditation to the Holy One. He breathed "*Alaha*" (Aramaic for "Sacred Unity" or the Holy One). Then he breathed "*Abwoon*" ("Father-Mother of the cosmos"). Finally, he got a "yes," although his breath was a bit mixed. It could go either way, really.

"My friend, are you sure about this? These bones could have been anyone—or anything. We don't know what will happen."

"We don't ever know what will happen, do we?" answered the fool. "I mean, you are always preaching that we shouldn't hold onto exalted states and experiences. Life is change. Become 'passers-through,' isn't that what I heard you tell Thomas?"

Issa couldn't argue with that. He turned his eyes inward and above, connected his breath again with that of the Holy Breath (in Aramaic, *ruha d'qoodsha*, usually translated "Holy Spirit"), and with one long, powerful exhalation, breathed into the pile of bones: "*Yyyhhhwwwhhh* . . . ."

In the next moment, the bones assembled themselves. Organs filled in, a heart started beating, flesh and hair formed around it all. It was a very large and—judging only by appearances rather than any animal communicator's method—angry lion.

The lion looked around quickly, saw Issa, saw the fool, and with one quick and powerful blow from its paw, took the top of the fool's head off. The fool's brain, according to Rumi anyway, rolled onto the earth, revealing itself to be smaller than a walnut. The fool, of course, fell over dead.

Issa was understandably shocked. He spoke to the lion courteously and said,

"O Lion, greetings of peace! Why did you take the top of this poor fool's head off?"

"For only one reason, O Ruh Allah," answered the lion, equally courteously, with mournful devotion in his eyes. "Because he was bothering you."

Issa paused to consider.

"Why then," he said, "don't you now consume what you've killed? That is normal for lions, isn't it? You don't waste anything."

"O Ruh Allah," replied the lion. "I lived my life to the full and ate everything allotted to me as written in the Book of Life. Nothing remains as my portion. Shortly said, I'm not hungry and can no longer be. I was happy on the other side until this fool brought you here. So my only wish is that you return me whence I've come."

"O Alaha," said Issa, sighing. Again, he turned within, focusing his heart's gaze on his connection with the One. Then he exhaled strongly, and re-inhaled the breath of life that he had given the lion, allowing its soul to return to the Holy Breath. The lion's body at once fell apart back into a pile of bones, just as it had been. The fool, of course, stayed dead.

That is the end of the story, beloveds. If it were your own inner story, the story of your inner life, who would be Issa? Who would be the fool and who the lion? And what part of you would need to die for you to know everything?

IV

Stories about Iblis

The Sufi stories about Iblis (a name sometimes mistranslated as *devil*) are some of the most edgy in our tradition.

If we take the basic premise of Sufi stories seriously—that all the actors and events exist within us, as reflections of the One Being's reality—then these stories challenge us with such questions as: What perverse part of me wants to forget about what really matters and sabotage my life? What voice inside would like to entice me to believe that I am the only thing that matters in the world and to act that way? Who is Iblis really, and what is the meaning of evil in the cosmos? Is a being like this inside of me or outside of me? A Sufi might say that there is only One Reality, so "inside" and "outside" are just limiting concepts of our own.

Even in the Hebrew Bible, we find evidence of an earlier, less theologized view of *satana*, the face of Reality that leads things astray or that tests someone with adversity.

One good example appears in the book of Job. Here *satana* clearly acts in agreement with the Holy One to test the unfortunate prophet. This would need to be true if what we mean by "God" were not some thought form or theological construct but the Reality behind the universe itself.

The Sufis say that the One created the universe because He/She/It was a "hidden treasure" and wanted to be known (this is one of the "sacred *hadith*" or sayings that came through the Prophet Muhammad). So, if we are part of an experiment in consciousness and free will—another word for creativity—then what role do behaviors like forgetting and making mistakes play?

Iblis's Refusal

The Iblis stories begin with the central one mentioned in the Qur'an and retold by Sufis through the ages. In some stories, Iblis is an angel. In others, he is a *jinn* (an Arabic word from which we indirectly receive the word "genie"), a being made of fire with powers over the elements as well as a certain amount of free will.

The following version is influenced by similar stories in Jewish *midrash* (commentary) and storytelling traditions as well as accounts in the Qur'an about God creating the first human being. As a matter of accuracy, the Qur'an presents the notion of "hell" as a place or state of reality found after death intended for purification. This purification can last a long time (given that time itself is a human construct) but doesn't last forever. Repeatedly, the Qur'an says that we all return to Allah *together*. So that's a bit different from the usual Christian concept of hell.

Here is how the central story goes:

Allah creates the human being and presents it to the angels and jinn:

"Behold! Here is my newest experiment in consciousness. It includes the awareness of all the experiments that have gone before it—minerals, plants, animals, stars, planets. But unlike those, it has freedom of action and will. It even has the freedom to forget that there is only one Reality behind the whole cosmos. At the same time, it has the potential, as much as any single created being can have, to reflect the awareness of the whole of Being. So, it can benefit the growth and evolution of everything, together *with* the rest of nature created before it. (Genesis 1:26–27 clearly says in Hebrew 'ruling *with*' all the other beings created before us, not *over* as usually mistranslated.)

"I offered the opportunity for this type of consciousness to the mountains, but they refused it. They just wanted to be mountains, without the freedom to forget Unity. Same thing with the plants and animals I previously created. Only the human being agreed to the job description and signed the 'contract.'

"I know we have discussed whether this is a good idea or not; however, it seems that it has only created arguments among you. I have judged that there will be more ripeness than unripeness involved, more good than evil. Anyway, I have gone ahead and created the human being. Here it is!

"So now, bow down to this new creation! It has a particle-formed body and you angels and jinn don't, so it is a more advanced model."

All the angels and jinn bowed down. All except Iblis, that is, who refused.

"O Allah, you created me of fire and this thing is only created of clay. Why should fire bow down to clay?"

"Iblis, I know what you don't. For your pride and insubordination, I am placing you in charge of the purification facility in the cosmos, which is for those who have the same pride of separating themselves from Me. This purification facility will have plenty of fire involved. In fact, the effects of the unripe actions of those in your 'sauna' will feed the fire until their pride and egotism are sweated out. For some, this may take a very long time."

"Okay," said Iblis, "but I will also do my best to entice as many as I can to what you call my prideful sense of separation, the illusion that the individual ego is the only thing that exists or that matters in the world. So the purification facility will be very busy."

"Nothing happens without my knowing," replied Allah. "Do your best. It will be a reality check on the experiment."

Iblis's Refusal, Take 2

The story of Iblis refusing to bow down to the First Human became a recurring theme of meditation and commentary for many classical Sufi poets and teachers.

The 9th-century Sufi Mansur Al-Hallaj offers what amounts to an apology for Iblis in his short collection of essays called *The Tawasin*.

Iblis, said Al-Hallaj, was overcome with love for Allah and couldn't bear to bow down to anything other than Allah. He was like an ascetic who just wanted to be alone in a cave, in unity with Unity. This seductive isolation led him to become attached to his own spiritual state.

Iblis argues with Allah this way:

"When I said that I was better than Adam, this was because I had served you longer. No one knows you better than I do. And anyway, given that there is only one Reality, from the beginning of time your intention was in my own, and mine was in yours.

"Therefore, whether I bowed down to Adam or not, it would still be necessary for me to return to the First Beginning, the place before all this *either-or*. Therefore, since my origin was the element of fire, I would end up in the fire anyway. Which is where I am.

"Nearness and distance are all one in You. In Unity there are no opposites. Likewise, desertion and companionship. So your deserting me and my love for you still create a unity."

Later the prophet *Musa* (Moses) met Iblis on the slope of Mount Sinai.

"Why didn't you just prostrate yourself, Iblis?" asked Musa. "It would have been so much easier."

"Several reasons," replied Iblis. "I declared that Allah was my Unique and Only Beloved. And I stuck by that declaration, even though I was asked to bow to Adam thousands of times."

"But you refused a direct command from Allah. Wasn't that a sin?" asked Musa.

"It was not a command, it was a test," replied Iblis.

"If it had been a test," countered Musa, "why did you suffer the punishment of being so deformed? I can hardly bare to look at you!" (In many of the Iblis traditions, his face was deformed from his refusal to bow down to the First Human.)

"One's spiritual state does not rely on outer appearances, Musa. You should know that. These outer changes don't affect what was there *in the Beginning*—that is, before the creation."

"So do you always remember Allah now?" asked Musa.

"What do remembrance or forgetfulness mean?" asked Iblis. "In the pure mind of Being, neither exists. There is no memory. Allah's remembrance is my remembrance, and vice versa. Can two be other than one?

"If Allah punishes me with fire for all eternity, I still would not bow down to anyone or anything, because I don't recognize any opposite to Allah. I am one of those who remain most true and sincere in love."

Iblis's Refusal, Take 3

From logic, of course, Hallaj's apology for Iblis makes a very seductive argument. Jelaluddin Rumi, however, looks at the story a bit differently and gives this version.

After being exiled to run the purification facility, Iblis appeals to Allah:

"O Allah, you have created everything and every situation. You created me. You tempted me. Now you've cursed me. You've known everything all the time. With you being omniscient and omnipotent, I had no choice. I was only following your plan, right?"

Rumi comments that this type of circular logic maybe irrefutable, but it is very impolite. He compares it to a short story of Adam after the first human was banished from the garden.

"Adam," asked God, "why didn't you argue with me along the lines that Iblis did? He said, for instance, 'You made me, you know all, and whatever you want to happen will happen.' You had a good case, too, but you didn't make it. Why?"

"Yes, I know," replied Adam, "but I could not forget my *adab* (courtesy and respect) in your presence. It would be talking like a lawyer. A lover doesn't speak this way to his or her Beloved."

Rumi goes on to say that remembrance and forgetfulness both have a place in the Holy One's universe. These opposites create new ways for Unity to experience Itself:

Constant remembrance of divine Unity,
the ecstasy of divine Love—
this creates heaven for us every moment.
If that's all we had,
we would all already be gone.
Why stay?
But we are meant to stay here for a time.
So we live with both
remembrance and forgetfulness,
Like the good cop and the bad cop on the beat.

Iblis's Refusal, Take 4

There are more variations on all of this.

For instance, Allah asked Iblis, the angels, and the jinn to bow down to the First Human, it's true. But that is because Allah wanted to hide the secret of how the human being would be brought to life from a lump of clay.

According to one account, Allah not only breathed into the clay, but also had some of the angels sing to intoxicate the soul or individual consciousness into entering the body. I suppose it would be a good feat . . . the angels singing while bowing down. But remember, this is a story. According to Sufis, from this first "singing" we receive our love of music.

In his epic poem *The Conference of the Birds,* a wonderful collection of interlinked Sufi stories, the 12th-century Sufi Fariduddin Attar gives us a different take on this part of the Iblis story:

Iblis knew that the Holy One was going to activate the human being and wanted to know the secret.

So he lined up just behind an angel, and as everyone went to bow, placing their wings on where their knees would be (if they had knees), Iblis went only part of the way down. Peering around the angel in front, he looked out of the corner of his eye to catch the secret. And he did! But Allah caught him doing it.

"Iblis, because of this pride, not only will you oversee the fiery sauna, but your name will be cursed by every human being who ever lives."

"That's all right," said Iblis. "What do I care if people mention my name? The more they mention me, the more they invoke me, and so the more present I'll be for them. As they say, bad publicity is better than none."

The last part of the story reminds me of the saying of the modern Sufi Inayat Khan: "Lull the devil to sleep rather than awaken him." And as one of his students, Murshid Samuel L. Lewis, once remarked, after a lifetime of working with his own inner contradictions, "In my life, God and the devil are on the same side." This doesn't mean that there is no unripeness in the world, or that we don't need to deal with it. But it does mean that we must first deal with the very subtle feelings of separation and pride that we carry within us.

Stories from Sa'adi

Sa'adi of Shiraz (1208–1291) wrote many charming love poems as well as collections of stories and short essays, much of the latter in the form of advice for rich merchants and rulers. He is best known for his collections of poetry and essays titled *The Gulistan* (Rose Garden) and *The Bustan* (Flower Garden).

Placing these in context, one needs to remember that, at that time in Persia and in the ancient world in general, "government" was arbitrary—that is, it was at the whim of the monarch. What we call the "rule of law" was nonexistent. A ruler might choose to adhere to the general principles of the Qur'an, but this was hardly certain. The same was true in the case of Christian, Buddhist, Hindu, or any other rulers. Buddhism along the Silk Road in the ancient world, for instance, was often very warlike. In any case, a ruler employed his or her own legal experts to interpret religious and ethical principles to the ruler's best advantage.

Sa'adi was fortunate to have the ear of several rulers in Persia without ever being an official "court poet" or functionary, which was often a life-threatening position (if the ruler were having a bad day). Sa'adi's love poetry, which deals with the beauty of human love, does not survive translation from Persian very well. Differing from Rumi, Sa'adi implies rather than teaches the significance of human, erotic love for mystical or divine love (if, in fact, there *is* a difference).

Likewise, many of his satirical pieces could take their place alongside those of great humorists like Mark Twain. Again, the colloquial references do not translate well. If you have a Persian friend, ask him or her to read you some Sa'adi in the original language.

I have included renditions of a few of Sa'adi's stories, extracted from various writings, where they are embedded in a tapestry of aphorisms, poetry, and practical advice for living. Hopefully, they will offer some of the delightful flavor of his wry way of looking at the world.

Advice for People in Business and Positions of Power

FALLING OFF THE CAMEL

Sa'adi relates:

Once I was the guest of a very successful businessman. He owned hundreds of slaves and camels, and he took me to his opulent home on the shore of the Persian Gulf. There he regaled me with all the important business contacts that he had made over the years and with how he planned to make money from his land and multiply his various investments. Really, I couldn't get a word in edgewise.

Then he began to speculate about the future business trips he might make: the relative risks and benefits, the distances and discomforts of the journeys, and the profits he could gain.

Finally, he said, "You know, Sa'adi, there is one trip I would like to make which would be the be-all-and-end-all. Once I did this, that would be it. I would retire in peace."

"What might that be?" I asked, eager to bring the conversation to a close so that I could go to bed.

"It's only this," he said. "I would take sulphur from Persia to China, where I could sell it for a profit. Then I would buy Chinese porcelain–dishes and vases–and bring them to Greece. They will fetch a lot there. Then in Greece I would buy fine brocade cloth, which I could take to India for a huge killing. With the profit, I would buy Indian metals, which I would take to Spain . . . ."

He went on like this for another half hour of buying and selling, concluding with: "Then I would return to Persia, sell what I had left, and settle down once and for all near my shop. What do you recommend, Sa'adi?"

All I could say tell him was:

"Once upon a time I heard that a businessman fell off his camel in the middle of the desert. He pulled himself to his feet, shook himself off, and shouted, to no one in particular:

'Only two things can satisfy
a greedy person's eyes:
hopeless contentment in Allah
or the dust of the grave.'"

A QUESTION OF ANTICIPATION AND VALUE

Sa'adi relates:

I once heard an Arab traveler tell the following story to a group of jewelers in Basra:

"A few years ago, I lost my way in the desert. I gave up hope for any deliverance but saw in the distance an oasis. Probably a mirage, I thought. But when I arrived, there was, in fact, actual water.

"I was saved but still very hungry. Behind one of the palm trees, I found a large sack that was very heavy. I jumped for joy, as I thought that it must be roasted wheat or rice that some caravan had left behind.

"Imagine my bitter disappointment when I opened the sack and found that it contained nothing but pearls."

THE CRAFTY SLAVE

Sa'adi relates:

Once upon a time, a slave ran away from the king's court. He was caught and returned. One of the viziers, who had never liked him in the first place, arranged for the slave to be sentenced to death. Normally, however, running away was not a capital offense in that kingdom.

The slave was asked for any last words, and he pleaded to take his case to the king himself.

"Yes?" asked the king. "I don't see how I can help you. You were in the vizier's charge and so are in his power."

"My liege," said the slave, "everything that is done in your kingdom is yours. You receive the benefit and you take the blame. My request is that you allow my execution to be legal, because right now it isn't. The Qur'an does not allow execution of slaves, except in the case of the crime of murder. I just want to make sure that the guilt for my death is not on your head on the Day of Judgment."

The king considered, scratching his beard. "How could I make it legal?"

"That's easy," said the slave. "Just allow me to kill the vizier. Then my execution will be perfectly legal."

"Hmm," said the king, and turning to the vizier: "What do you say to this?"

The vizier gulped. "I yield, my liege. The slave can go free."

"All right," the king said to him. "Before you line up against an enemy, you had better accurately estimate that person's real ability; otherwise you're done for."

LIKE FOR LIKE

Sa'adi relates:

I've also heard tell that once, in the court of the great Sultan Harun al-Rashid, the sultan's son came running into the throne room with an urgent complaint.

"What is it, my son?" asked Harun al-Rashid.

"A disreputable, lower-class person, someone of the street, has just insulted my mother, your wife. What should I do? Can't I kill him?"

Harun al-Rashid asked his advisers what they recommended. Most of them recommended death, with the boy nodding in agreement. The sultan listened to them all and then pondered for a moment.

"Death is not an option," he decreed. "The Qur'an doesn't allow it for mere defamation. The one solution I can see is for you, son, to insult his mother in return. But only to the same degree or less, not more. The Qur'an allows this in the case of an offense: to return like (or preferably less) for like.

"If it's more, then you will be the offender and judged that way on the Last Day. An equal insult is, of course, very difficult to estimate. All in all, it's much wiser to forgive than to try to exact an 'eye for an eye.'"

JUST PASSING THROUGH

Sa'adi relates:

I also heard that a wandering dervish once entered the palace of King Ibrahim Adham of Balkh (in present-day Afghanistan), who later gave up his throne to become a dervish himself.

The dervish began to unpack his small sack and make himself at home in a corner of the courtyard.

"Hey, you!" yelled a guard. "What do you think you're doing?"

"I'm staying for the night. This is a caravanserai, a place for passing travelers."

"This is no caravanserai–this is the king's palace," replied another guard. "Get out!"

"No, this is a caravanserai," said the dervish placidly.

After arguing with him for a bit, the guards took him to the king.

"Brother dervish, I've been told you think this is a caravanserai," said Ibrahim Adham. "Why?"

"Who was here before you?" asked the dervish.

"My father," the king replied.

"And before that?"

"My grandfather."

"And who will be here after you?"

"My son, I suppose. *Inshallah*."

"Then none of you are here permanently. You are only passing through. It's a caravanserai. I rest my case."

After that, Ibrahim Adham allowed the dervish to stay in the palace courtyard as long as he liked.

Advice for Lovers

TEMPTATION

Someone once asked me a theoretical question:

"If you were safely inside a room with a lovely beloved, the doors locked, all rivals safely out of the way or asleep, your heart anxious and passions high on both sides, could you refrain from indulging yourself by the power of your abstinence?"

"Maybe I could resist temptation," I replied, "but I would not, in any case, escape the gossip of the neighbors."

SURPRISED BY THE BELOVED

On one occasion I was surprised by my beloved, who entered my room while I was reading in bed. As I jumped out of bed and rushed to her, I accidentally brushed the candle with my sleeve and put it out.

"Where did *this* treasure come from?" I asked, embracing her warmly.

She shrugged me off and settled herself into a chair.

Then she retorted, "Why did you put out the light as soon as you saw me? Were you presuming?"

"Because I thought that the sun had come up," I replied quickly.

"Really?" she replied, exasperated. "Can't you do better than that?"

"All right. Men of wisdom have said, 'If boring people should enter the room and block the light, then give them the heave-ho. But if a stunningly beautiful, perceptive, charming one does, then take her around the waist and blow out the candle.' How's that?"

ABOUT LOVE AND PASSION

You may consider it a sin to look at a beautiful shape, but I count it one not to.

※

If it were not for beautiful shapes, love's mystery would never have been born.

If there were no roses, then we would never hear the nightingale's songs of joy and sorrow.

※

If the language of love makes no impression on your heart, then you are already as good as dead.

That's why I say: no matter how difficult, temperamental, and rude the object of your love may be, it is still better to carry on courting rather than deprive your heart of the exercise.

It is easier to bear adversity than live without love.

Nor is it the right behavior for a lover to bargain with the beloved. Give your heart without reserve, whether the response is harsh or kind. At the end, whenever and however that may be, at least you can say with some modesty:

"I have loved."

Moth and Candle: Two Points of View

Fariduddin Attar relates one version of this famous Sufi story in his poetic story-cycle titled *Mantiq ut-Tair* ("the conference of the birds"). Sa'adi switches the point of view and then offers some advice for the spiritual traveler.

⁂

First, in case you don't know it, here is a version of Attar's story. This more traditional one takes place from the moths' point of view:

One day a group of moths fell in love with a candle. But from from their viewpoint they couldn't see any details, only a blinding light. They consulted among themselves and decided to send one of their number to investigate their beloved more closely.

One moth went out and returned, then gave a more detailed description: flame, wax, sometimes smoke, some sizzling sounds. The moths had a leader, of course, like the shaykh of the moths. This wise moth, who chaired the meeting, decided the report wasn't good enough, so another moth volunteered to go.

The second moth singed its wings on the flame and returned. It described the burning sensation, the pain, and the intense heat. After consideration, the wise moth declared that this report was still incomplete.

Finally, a third moth flew right into the flame, embraced it, and made love to it. Flame and moth were one.

"This one truly knows and understands," commented the wise moth, "but it can't say anything."

※

Here is Sa'adi's version:

One night as I lay awake, I heard a moth and a candle talking together in the room next door, where some friends were sitting.

"Oh! I am *so* in love," said the moth, as it hovered around the flame enthusiastically. "Just *so* in love. I really deserve to be burnt, burnt to a cinder. But you, candle, why are you crying, why are you burning?"

"Yes, you say you're a lover," replied the candle dourly. "But I'm already burning and melting. I long for my original Beloved, the sweet honeycomb from which my wax was taken. She is still part of me, so I cry and burn. What you see running down my sides is the flood of pain engulfing my face.

"How can you call *yourself* a lover?" continued the candle. "You run around and around and away from the flame. I am standing here naked, being burnt, head to toe. Maybe love singes your wings. So what? Love is melting me from top to bottom."

The candle continued speaking this way most of the night.

After a while, some lovely person in the room called the meeting to a close, blew out the candle, and called,

"Good night, everyone!"

The candle's head was now in smoke, but it still spoke to the moth:

"This is the end of loving, my friend. But if you want to learn the way to love, then remember this: die to yourself and you will be saved from burning.

"Don't mourn the one who dies by the Beloved's hand. Rejoice that the Beloved has absorbed that lucky one into itself as the Friend."

VI

The Man of the Big Fish

In 1979, I was with a group of pilgrims in Lahore, Pakistan, visiting a Sufi shaykh who was also a coffee merchant. He invited us into his upper storage room for *dhikr*, the Sufi practice of "remembrance." This usually uses some chanted or silently breathed form of the phrase *la ilaha illa 'llah* (there is no reality but the One Reality) for contemplation.

The shaykh, however, introduced us to a *dhikr* that I had not heard before: a chant that the prophet Jonah used while in the belly of the whale. Later, I found that the Qur'an cites this *dhikr* (in Sura Al Anbiya), in relation to the "man of the big fish."

To add to this peculiarity, the small group of us sat on the floor in a circle around a large heap of coffee beans. We each repeated the chant to ourselves softly, and with each repetition, we pulled one coffee bean from the center and placed it in a small pile in front of us. When all the beans were gone, we pushed our small piles back in and started again. I can't remember how long this went on or how the practice ended, but the coffee afterward was very tasty!

With only a sentence or two in the Qur'an to go on, various Islamic and Sufi versions of the story of Jonah later arose. They don't all agree with one other. For instance, in some versions Jonah is a merchant; in others, a born prophet. The whale, of course, is always there. In all of the versions, God asks Jonah to preach to the people of Nineveh (near modern Mosul in northern Iraq, not coincidentally). At some point, he gets fed up. I have chosen the version I like best, which has something to do with how we deal with our expectations. Jonah's name in Arabic is *Yunus* (meaning "dove"), and so that's what I'll use in the story.

Young Jonah

Once upon a time in the Holy Land, a young boy was born to a family that had had several generations of seers in its lineage.

Now, in those days, a "prophet" or *nabi* (Hebrew, *nabiya*) did not mean someone who predicted the future. A prophet, by the literal meaning of the word, received something from the spirit world and then conveyed it for the benefit of the community. We might today call such people clairvoyant or clairaudient. Materialistic, unimaginative communities have also called such people schizophrenic, liminally challenged, or simply crazy. It seems important in such cases for there to be a community that supports the prophet and knows how to make the best use of his or her abilities. These abilities can range from checking a diagnosis of an illness to simply helping a person strengthen his or her own intuitive connection to the Holy One. The person-to-person relationship is a bit like putting two batteries together and doubling the intuitive current.

Back to our story: Young Yunus also showed signs of being open to "other worlds." Now some prophets *see* visually, whereas others experience a clear body awareness. The Bible, for instance, reports that many of the old Hebrew prophets experienced intense shaking before prophesying. For his part, Yunus heard things very clearly. His voice of intuition connected to the other world. Even as a boy, he could bring back guidance for anyone who came to him for healing or advice.

As he grew older, his family sent Yunus to apprentice with a prophet in a nearby village, a type of prophetic finishing school. By the time he was a young man, Yunus was comfortably installed as the prophet of his home village. Naturally, he received support from the village. In those days, a village that didn't have a prophet was not a real village (a bit like an English village today without a pub).

Yunus married and had two fine young boys. Everyone was happy.

The Mission

It just so happened that one day, while Yunus was in prayer and meditation (same word for both whether in Hebrew, Aramaic, or Arabic), he heard the *Bat Kol* (the voice of the Holy One) coming to him.

"Yunus," said the Holy One.

"Yes, see, here I am," answered Yunus.

"I have a mission for you."

"Very good. What is it?"

"I want you to take your family, leave your village, and move to Nineveh, preaching the message of Unity there."

A pause followed.

"Could you repeat that, please, Holy One?"

"You heard me the first time. I know these things."

"But Holy One! What will my village do without me? They need me!"

"I've already covered that through a boy named Basir in the lane next to yours. I've given him the Gift, too."

"But everyone knows me and my family here. This is our home. How can I take the boys out of school? What about my wife? What will we live on?"

"Do you trust the inner voice or not?"

Now his teacher had trained Yunus properly, and so he knew that not every voice that comes to a person is the Voice. As one of my Sufi teachers once said, "What makes you think that just because a person doesn't have a body he or she is any more truthful than one with a body?" In other words, there is a lot out there in the "other worlds" that is no less nonsense than in this one.

So Yunus practiced all the inner testing he had learned—breathing the unnamable Name, drawing its letters on the voice he heard, and so forth.

"Holy One, are you still there?"

"Yes, I'm waiting, Yunus. Do you agree or not?"

Yunus had no choice, so he agreed. If he refused, then he would lose the gift, because he would have cut off his channel to the Holy One. That's the way it works. But moving on . . . . I won't describe the scene that ensued when Yunus told his wife. There was some convincing to do. His two boys were easier . . . their response was a simple "Whatever!" Yunus made an announcement to his village (also informing them of his replacement), and the family made their goodbyes. They packed their belongings on a donkey and set out.

The Journey to Nineveh

Nineveh was a long distance away from where the family lived. By some accounts, Yunus' birthplace was a village a few kilometers north of the present-day city of Nazareth. So, the family traveled for a month before they reached the shore of the Tigris river, just west of Nineveh.

Fortunately, the river was in low ebb, but it was a wide river. Yunus found the narrowest place to ford, between two hills. He proposed to wade across with this older son on the donkey, then come back with the donkey for his wife and younger son. When they were halfway across, however, a sudden, intense rainstorm arose, and a wall of water—a flash flood—came rushing down the small gorge, engulfing both hills.

Yunus only had time to grab his son off the donkey and swim for their lives to the other side. They barely made it, since the distance was now much greater than before. Panting heavily, he dragged himself and his son onto the bank. Looking back, he could see that the rain was letting up and the flash flood was already subsiding. So Yunus told his son to wait on the shore, and he would go back for his brother and mother.

Crossing the river again, this time wading with difficulty, he began to walk back upstream on the other shore, since they had been washed quite a bit downstream by the flood. He walked and walked. The flood had changed the landscape so that, in an arid landscape, one small hill looked like another. After some hours, he still couldn't find his wife and younger son, or any sign of where they had been.

Yunus sat down on a rock and prayed.

"Holy One, what now?"

"Keep going. Don't worry."

"What? How can I go on without my wife and son?"

"They'll be fine. Keep going."

Yunus waded back to the other side and walked back downstream. But now he couldn't find his older son, either.

"Holy One, this is really not all right!"

"Keep going!"

Yunus continued and by evening found himself at the gates of Nineveh.

In ancient times, Nineveh was a very large city, the capital of old Assyria. Now this part isn't in the Bible, but generations before, Abraham (yes, *that* Abraham) had originally started out his prophetic career in Nineveh. He had been involved in a series of confrontations with the Assyrian king Nimrod. The issues were the usual: there is only one Reality, let's recognize it, and treat other people and the God's creation justly. (I won't go into all that here, since I already did so in *The Tent of Abraham*, which has some wonderful Sufi stories of Abraham.)

In short, the message that God sent Yunus to bring to the people of Nineveh was the same message Abraham had given and simple enough that they really should have remembered it. However, much time had gone by, and people had relapsed into the same cultural amnesia: great disparities between the very rich and very poor, everyone out for themselves, basic forgetfulness of the one Reality behind it all.

Yunus still had some money with him, so he rented a small room. "Well," he thought despairingly to himself, "I might as well start and get this over with. If they don't listen, then maybe I can go find my family and return home."

Yunus entered the central marketplace, which was very busy. He was from a small village, but nonetheless, since he had been trained properly, he could also use his voice to make people pay attention. He went to the central well, stood on the stones, and called out in a loud voice:

"Hey, Ninevites! The Holy One has sent me to you with a message. Start acknowledging there is only one Reality—*la ilaha illa 'llah*—and start treating the poor among you properly!"

A few people around him stopped for an instant, then quickly went back to what they were doing. Crazy people often came to the marketplace, they thought. Usually, if you didn't pay them any attention, they went away.

"Hey, Ninevites! Listen up! There is a greater Reality in the cosmos than just buying and selling. Look around you! Can't you see? Come to your senses and start acting like human beings!"

"He speaks in complete sentences, I'll give him that," said one merchant to another.

"Yes, makes a nice change," his friend replied. "I also like the sound of his voice, very resonant. Obviously well trained."

The day went on, and Yunus continued with variations on the same message. A few people began to gather around and listen. However, when they did, they also began heckling him.

"Who did you say sent you? The Holy One? What 'holy one'? The only holey one I know is my roof."

"We've never seen you before. You can't be from around here! Foreigner!"

"Go away, you're ruining our business! Go to some other town where they're more gullible."

Yunus continued and people began to take aim at him with whatever soft fruit or past-their-prime vegetables were at hand. Things were not going well.

At the end of the day, Yunus returned to his room and opened a channel to the Holy One.

"Not so good, Holy One. What now?"

"Keep at it. They'll come around."

Yunus sighed. The next day was the same as the first—except that the fruit and vegetables started a bit earlier. The following day was the same. And the next, and the next.

Yunus tried to change the sound of his voice. Perhaps more pathos or enthusiasm or even good humor. He tried using stories, analogies, catchy rhyming slogans, or even philosophical syllogisms. People were initially intrigued by the changes, but the fruit and vegetables eventually arrived. After a while, no matter what he did, no one was listening.

"They're not listening, Holy One."

"Keep at it. They'll come around."

Yunus did keep at it for six months, but at the end of that time, he was in despair.

"What am I doing wrong, Holy One? I've tried everything I know. I don't know what to do next."

"Try this. Tell them that if they don't listen. I'm going to send the *Fire*."

"The Fire? Any other details I can offer?"

"Just the *Fire*. That's enough."

Yunus tried it. As it would today, yelling the word "Fire!" in a crowded marketplace did have some effect.

"Who's sending fire? Some arsonist? What are you, a terrorist?"

"Who is this Holy One, after all? Just a figment of your imagination, really."

"We've gotten used to you, friend. We like your face, but seriously, you need psychological help!"

Yunus kept at it, but after some weeks, they were just ignoring him again. Or throwing fruit and vegetables.

"What now, Holy One?"

"Give them a time limit. Let's say a month. If there is no response in a month, I'm sending the Fire."

Yunus tried it. Getting more specific did draw some people's attention.

"Look, you seem to be a sensible and intelligent person," said one man. "But what are you really on about? There must be something to what you're saying if you can keep at it all these months."

Yunus began to explain to him the way life was supposed to work for the best happiness of all, do unto others, and so forth . . . one Life behind all. After about an hour with Yunus in private conversation, the man said, "I'll think about it" and walked away. But the next day, Yunus didn't see him again.

The month went by slowly in the same fashion. A little interest, but mostly boredom, insults, and fruit. Yunus couldn't wait for it to end. Finally, after the last day, Yunus left the city gates and sat on a small hill. He opened his hotline to the Holy One.

"Okay, that's it. Bring the Fire!"

"But you've had a bit of interest. Some of those to whom you talked did listen, and I can see they're turning it over in their hearts. You never know."

"Look, Holy One! With all due respect, you said you'd send the Fire after a month. The month is gone. If you don't, and I go back tomorrow, they'll just laugh at me. 'Why aren't we toast, Yunus?' I can hear it now."

"Yunus, I never said it would be easy. It's the nature of prophets to suffer rejection and to feel the disunity around them intensely. One needs more patience and fewer expectations."

"Okay, I've heard it all before. If that's the nature of prophets, then I quit! I am turning in my prophet's license. I don't care if I lose my gift, and we never speak again!"

The Big Fish

Yunus turned his back on Nineveh and stomped away back into the desert. He was so angry that at first he didn't know where he was going, just as far away from Nineveh as he could get. He had lost his family, his vocation, and his livelihood.

When he came to himself, he decided to head north, maybe to reach the sea and sail far away. As luck would have it, he met a caravan heading north and joined up with it. When they reached the Black Sea, Yunus found passage as a deckhand on one of the ships sailing west.

All was going well. Maybe he could stay on board and work for the ship owner when they reached port. He would always be on the move, never accountable to anyone!

However (as most of you know), as luck—or something else—would have it, a large storm came up about a day out of port. At first, Yunus joined the rest of the crew and worked harder to keep the ship afloat. But the storm went on for a day and a night. Now the captain of the ship was a superstitious man, or perhaps he had a sixth sense.

"Is anyone here carrying some bad luck?" he yelled over the storm. "Anyone commit sacrilege against any god or goddess whatsoever in the last month? Speak now! I have charms and herbs with me in my cabin, and we can brew up something. Anything! We can't hold out in this storm much longer, and it doesn't seem to be letting up."

Yunus at first ignored the announcement. He didn't believe in any of that nonsense anymore. But as the storm raged on, he began to pray inwardly—and then he stopped. What was he doing? He came to a difficult decision.

"Captain, it's me."

"Okay, whom did you offend?" asked the captain. "I have a whole chest full of protective charms."

"I don't think they will work. I turned my back on the Ruler and Substance of the entire universe, the Being behind all of the manifest and unmanifest worlds, not just some local god or goddess."

"Oh. Any suggestions?"

"Better throw me overboard. I lost my family and work and have no reason to live anymore. So at least I can save all of you."

The captain and crew consulted (albeit quickly). They had never thrown a crew member overboard before (except in the case of mutiny, insubordination, or in only one case, extreme and perverse laziness). As the storm continued, however, they helped Yunus over the side. As he went down, he called out inwardly to the Holy One for forgiveness.

Cutting to the best part: A whale swallowed Yunus and (don't ask me how, it's a story, after all!) he awoke inside the whale. (If you want speculative anatomical details concerning a whale or fish large enough to swallow a man without chewing, then you will need to go online. We don't concern ourselves with these things here.)

"O Holy One, thank you!" sighed Yunus. "At least here, I can repent and say your name for a short time. Before I'm digested." Yunus breathed and reopened the channel he knew so well and heard this as the chant he should do:

La ilaha illa anta subhanaka
Inni kuntu min az-zalamin

When you hear something inside the belly of a whale, you usually don't question it or try to take apart the meaning very deeply. It was generally in the form of a chant that he had often done but with many differences. At first, the meaning seemed clear:

There is no god except You,
the only one to be praised,
and I'm indeed in this very deep and dark place
because I messed up very badly.

As the hours went by, Yunus also began to hear the meaning of the words of the chant differently. (Semitic languages allow for this "deeper hearing.") The Arabic words could also be interpreted this way:

There is no reality or anything worth considering but You,
the purity that every being experiences in the first
Beginning.
Really! I was coming at things from
an egotistic, rigid idea of fulfilling my human purpose.
My own soul is only the depth
of your divine breath and your divine image.

Yes, thought Yunus. *Separation from the One. Rigid ideas about the way things should be, rather than the way they are. That's always been the problem, but I only preached it to others, I didn't experience it myself.*

Forty days and nights went by. Now this could be a symbolic number, but recent research shows it usually takes six weeks to change a habit pattern in one's nervous system, whether of action or thought. And remember, it's a story, which is more about you than about a person named Yunus.

As you may know, this whale was a vegetarian (look it up—most of the largest ones are). So, without grounding itself, the whale belched up Yunus close enough to the shore that he could easily make it. Panting, he pulled himself onto the beach and praised the One.

At this point, according to most sources, God caused a large gourd plant (maybe a Middle Eastern pumpkin) to grow up overnight, sheltering Yunus from the sun until he was ready to continue. In the biblical story, the gourd comes up at a different point in the story and then dies suddenly (still a lesson about nonattachment). Here it seems to say to Yunus, "Hey, things can change quickly!"

Return to Nineveh

Yunus was very tired and hungry, but as if by magic, a fisherman and his family found and cared for him. After he recuperated a bit, they told him where he was, which was on the southwestern shore of the sea. He headed back east toward Nineveh and found his way to the trail that he had originally taken all those months ago.

Since the Tigris River was again at low ebb, he even found his way back to the same spot where he and his family had tried to cross. Something made him sit down on the hill and rest a bit. In about five minutes, a small boat came upstream rowed by an Assyrian peasant. Yunus' wife and younger son were in the stern of the boat!

"Praise the One! Where were you, what happened to you? I thought you were dead," cried Yunus.

"We were swept away far downstream by the flood," replied his wife, "but by chance, we landed on the opposite shore. This blessed fisherman and his son saved us. His family has cared for us all these months. But one of his daughters seems to have a vocation like yours, as a prophetess. She told us that today was the day to come back upstream to try to find you."

The fisherman carried the three of them to the other side, where they disembarked and prepared to start for Nineveh. However, as it just so happens, at that moment, over a nearby sand dune appeared a camel ridden by a Bedouin, with Yunus' elder son riding behind him.

Yes, it was a similar story. The boy had waited for his father a long time and then wandered into the desert and gotten lost. He was saved by a Bedouin tribe, which also had a soothsayer (as any self-respecting tribe would), who told him not only the day and time, but also the exact location to which to return.

It was, in fact, a miracle (or two, really). The family continued to Nineveh. When Yunus arrived, he and his family were walking through the marketplace when one of the people with whom he'd had a longer talk stopped him.

"Where have you been, Yunus? I've missed you. Over all these months, I've thought about what you said, and I agree that you're right. If I look around, at the sun and the moon and the stars, and, well, everything, I can only conclude that there must be some larger Being and purpose behind it all. Like the regular journey of the stars, I also must have a proper role to play. . . . Is this your family? They look fine, but you look awful! Why don't you come to my house and meet my wife and family? No place to stay? No problem. We have an extra room where you can stay as long as you wish."

Now I could tell you that Yunus lived happily ever after, and that the next day everyone in Nineveh acknowledged the One Reality and everything changed for the better overnight. But that would be too much, even for a story like this.

Yunus carried on with prophesying and found work helping his new friend with his caravan business, import-export. He slowly gathered a small circle of people who started to change the way they lived to be in harmony with a bigger picture of life.

And Yunus understood that, in this life, a picture moves and changes as it is being painted, just as did the image of the Holy One in his soul.

That could be the end of the story, except for one more small linguistic point. The name *Nineveh* in Aramaic (its native language, after all) seems to derive from the word for *fish*. So, who or what swallowed Yunus?

VII

A Sufi Fairy Tale

Some Sufi stories could easily appear in a collection by the Brothers Grimm or Hans Christian Andersen. In them you might find oppressed princesses, heroic princes, poor families discovering a fortune, improbable shifts of time and space, and magical interventions by disembodied voices or entities.

If you delve into the classic European fairy tales, however, you will see that the versions we usually tell children or depict in Hollywood films present a much tamer story than the originals; they have been "disinfected" of all their violent and disturbing elements. Modern psychologists have argued that we have done ourselves a disservice in so doing, since children are more than willing to face both the light and dark sides of life in story form. They sense life's dangers around them anyway (through their parents' anxiety if nothing else), but they don't have a framework for making sense of it. A fairy story can offer that. Also, as we are finding today with the overuse of household disinfectants, which seem to compromise our immune systems, it may be healthier to allow a certain amount of "germ-life" to coexist with us rather than to try make everything antiseptically pure. In short, life is complicated and seldom lends itself to simple, idealized solutions.

Going further, various Jungian and other archetypal psychologists have had a field day with the German *märchen*, trying to squeeze every element of a fairy tale into this or that personality theory, much like the ugly sisters trying to squeeze their feet into Cinderella's slipper. I'm not saying that these stories don't have a deep effect on the psyche, but they function better if you simply allow them to work on their own without trying to use the logical mind to understand areas of oneself that are more wild and untamed than any theory can explain.

The following story does have some similarities to "Cinderella," but this version comes from Persia. I find it more fun and earthy, not relying so much on magic. The heroine is her own fairy godmother, and the prince does not seem very bright. Psychologists—enjoy yourselves!

The Lady and the Golden Lampstand

Once upon a time, a rich merchant lived in old Isfahan, and after his wife died, he became increasingly greedy. He rattled around in his extremely large house and neglected his only child, a daughter. Out of greed or sheer perversity, he decided to marry her off to a rich friend, a much older merchant with whom he wanted to curry favor.

The young woman refused point-blank, but in that society at that time, daughters had very few rights. Her father shut her up in the house and refused to let her go out for fear that she might meet someone, much less a someone with whom she might want to run off.

The daughter continued to argue, but her father wouldn't be moved. Finally, the daughter asked that her father at least grant her one wish before she married his odious friend. She wanted a large golden lampstand constructed for her room. It needed to be large enough to hold forty candles. Since her father had plenty of money and wanted to end her complaining, he agreed.

The young woman, whose name was Farida, went to the local goldsmith and gave him specific instructions. The lampstand needed to be the size of a very large tree in girth. Yes, big enough outside to hold forty large candles around its perimeter. But it should also be hollow inside, large enough to hold several small rooms and a bed. (Maybe the size of a giant redwood tree?) The door should be able to be locked from the inside and completely invisible from the outside. (You can see where this is going.) The goldsmith agreed, and after a short time, the lampstand was installed in Farida's room.

As the date for the wedding neared, Farida began to stockpile food in the lampstand. Soon she had enough for four months. Then one day while her father was out, she went to the well in their courtyard. She left her shoes by the side of it with one of her dresses draped over the edge. Then she shut herself inside the lampstand and locked the door.

When her father returned home, he looked all over the house for her. Finally, he saw her shoes and dress near the well. Not bothering to look inside the well, he assumed that she had drowned herself out of despair. He mourned (briefly) but didn't tell anyone. After about a month, he decided to get rid of the golden lampstand. It reminded him of his daughter, and of course, of his own guilt, which he still didn't admit to himself. He had the lampstand taken to the local auctioneer to be sold. The father leaves our story here.

As it so happened, on the day that the lampstand was being auctioned off, a prince from a nearby city was passing through. He saw the lampstand and for some unknown reason felt that he must have it. He bid much higher than anyone else, and when he returned home, he had it installed in his own rooms at the palace.

All of this was completely out of character. The prince was, to this point, what we might call an introvert and a creature of habit, especially in terms of his meals. He preferred to eat alone. When his evening meal was delivered to his rooms, he would always eat part of it and then save the rest for breakfast. That way he wouldn't need to see anyone until lunch.

One morning, the prince noticed that the food that was left for breakfast seemed to be a bit less than what he had left the night before. But he concluded this must be his imagination. The next morning there seemed to be even less. So, he decided to try to stay awake to see what was happening. Before bed, he cut his finger slightly and put some salt on the wound to keep himself awake. (Don't try this at home!)

Around midnight, he saw a beautiful woman gliding out of the golden lampstand, and as the storytellers say, she was "shining like the sun at night." With one eye open, he watched her eat from his dinner and then return inside the lampstand. Well, as the storytellers also say, the prince was smitten.

He decided to repeat the procedure the next night. The same thing happened. After that, he was fully in love.

On the third night, the lampstand opened again at midnight, and Farida emerged. After she had eaten from his bowl, she was about to return to the lampstand when he jumped up and caught her hand.

I must apologize for the improbability, but the storytellers also say that Farida had also fallen in love with the prince over the weeks she had been observing him covertly. I should have said something before now, but that's the way these stories go.

The two decided to keep the whole thing secret. They would spend the day apart and all night together. And so they did—talking, eating together, making love, and generally enjoying each other's company. All of this could have gone on very happily for the rest of the story, except for one thing.

The prince had been promised to his cousin, the daughter of his uncle, the king's brother.

One night, one of the palace handmaidens (who seem to be everywhere in these stories) heard talking and laughter coming from the prince's rooms early in the morning. When she peeped through the keyhole, she saw the prince with a beautiful young woman. Naturally, word spread among the handmaiden sorority until it reached the ears of the handmaiden of the prince's cousin, who promptly told her mistress. She dispatched her handmaiden to peer through the keyhole all night and find out where the strange woman came from. The unfortunate handmaiden certainly got a neckache doing so, but she succeeded in discovering the secret of the golden lampstand. After this was reported to the cousin, she decided to take matters into her own hands.

One day when the prince was out hunting (which seems to be the main occupation of princes in these types of stories), the cousin asked the king to allow her to borrow the lampstand for a reception she was offering in her part of the palace that day. The king at first refused, since the prince had given specific instructions that the lampstand was not to be touched by anyone. However, his niece was so persistent that he finally gave in. What harm could there be?

When the lampstand was brought to the cousin's rooms, she at once ordered forty candles to be installed and lit on it. Slowly the whole lampstand became hotter and hotter. Farida endured as long as she could, but finally she burst out of the lampstand, burnt and blistered. She ran out, jumped into a tank of water outside the cousin's rooms and promptly passed out. Since the cousin thought she must be dead, she had her wrapped in a felt carpet liner and thrown into the moat around the palace.

As it so happened, an old palace retainer was returning to his hut at the time and heard groaning sounds coming from the moat. When he fished out the rolled-up carpet liner, he found a young woman inside. He took Farida home and slowly nursed her back to health. Her wounds took a while to heal, and due to the trauma, she couldn't really remember what had happened or who she was. Since the old retainer's wife had died some years before, and he had no children, he adopted Farida as his own daughter (informally, of course; please remember the fairy-tale judicial system!).

Back to the prince: When he returned from hunting, he found the golden lampstand back in his rooms, but with the door open and no one inside. No one would tell him anything about what had happened, because they were all too frightened what might happen to them. The prince, for his part, was not very proactive and collapsed from grief and shock. He began to waste away. As he was the king's only heir, this became a major emergency.

The king dispatched the usual physicians to investigate and propose a cure. One—a bit more perceptive than most—diagnosed that the prince was lovesick. Nothing would cure him except for the sight of his beloved. What to do?

Fortunately, the king had a wise vizier rather than a rotten one (which can also happen in such stories). The vizier put out a proclamation that all the people of the city, rich and poor, should cook a dish for the king's son. Perhaps that would tempt him to eat and build up his resources. Lateral thinking, that!

As the prince continued to waste away, the townspeople began to bring their best and tastiest dishes, which were (of course) refused. When news of the proclamation reached the old retainer, he related it to Farida.

The mention of "food" and "prince" together seemed to spark her memory. She asked her adopted father to go to the market to buy a bit of barley flour. With the flour, she made some noodles and put them into a stew composed of mixed vegetables and small pieces of lamb. (The Persians call this simple dish an *ash*.) Farida poured the stew into a simple earthenware bowl and in the bottom placed a ring that the prince had given her as a token of his love. Yes, we didn't know about the ring, but it makes an opportune appearance here.

You can guess what happens next. When he walked up to the palace, all the guards laughed at the old man, bearing his simple stew in a simple bowl.

"Don't break my heart!" exclaimed the old man. "Yes, I am poor, but this is the best I have. And the vizier did say, 'rich and poor.'"

When the prince saw the old man, his heart was moved and he tasted a spoonful of *ash*. Then another. And another. Perhaps there was some strange link between the prince's appetite and his memory of his beloved. Or maybe he sensed her touch or fragrance in the chopped vegetables! We won't speculate further. In any case, food was the trigger, and he continued eating. Finally, he reached the bottom of the bowl and found the ring. That did it. He asked the old retainer who had cooked the stew, and everything came out.

The now-revived prince sent royal messengers to bring Farida to the palace. He apologized profusely for not searching for her (as well he should have). The nefarious cousin was disgraced, order was restored, and shortly afterward a royal wedding took place. Farida's adopted father, the old retainer, also came to live with the couple in the palace. Now there was no need to hide in a golden lampstand, since the couple's love was out in the open.

We can hope that the prince's character improved so that when he became king he ruled wisely (fortunately, he had Farida to rely on). Nevertheless, the storytellers don't go into what happened next. All they tell us is that, just after the wedding, the prince ordered new street lighting for all forty towns in his realm, as a tribute to his wife, the lady of the golden lampstand. It was a start, anyway!

VIII

From the Arabian Nights: The Hunchback of Ch'ang-an

I've adapted this story from one in the "One Thousand and One Arabian Nights," a collection that in fact includes only 271 nights in the original version. The number in the Arabic title meant to refer to an unspecified, very large number (like an American saying "a gazillion nights"). Not understanding this, various translators added more stories to later versions to try to make up the numbers literally.

Here is the basic "frame story" in case you don't know it.

King Shahrayar has been betrayed in love by his wife (which is also a long story) and so won't spend any more than one night with a mistress. It's an old yet modern story. He just doesn't want to get involved and hurt again. Now, please allow for that arbitrary quality of government

I mentioned earlier. Absolute power corrupts, and so forth. Being a king, he had each mistress executed the morning after. An extreme way not to get attached, you might say. But remember . . . it's only a story!

The latest potential victim, Shahrazad, gets around the difficulty by telling the king a story each night after they make love, a story that she stops in the middle. You could say that Shahrazad was the first real master of the cliff-hanger. Many of the stories she tells are stories within stories, which is a wonderful insurance policy. Also, the tone and genre change within and between stories. Some are comic, some tragic, some erotic, some folktales, some teaching stories, and some what we would now call "shaggy dog" stories.

The story retold here is what we might call a "shaggy-dog dark comedy," although it comes out all right in the end. Believe it or not, I have simplified the story quite a bit, so Shahrazad must have had a remarkable imagination as well as an excellent memory.

Some of the oddities of the story, like the prominent position of various religious minorities in Chinese culture and the imperial court, have a basis in fact.

In the early eighth century CE, the emperor of the T'ang dynasty took an unusually keen interest in foreign religions and esoteric exotica. For instance, he often sought out Manicheans and Nestorian Christians as astrologers or healers. One priest claimed to be able to chant people to death and then revive them. A Buddhist monk claimed to be two hundred years old and have the secret to the elixir of immortality. The emperor was fascinated with all this sort of thing.

At that time, the capital was not in Beijing, but in the far western part of China at the eastern end of the Silk Road, a city then called Ch'ang-an (the modern-day X'ian). Ch'ang-an became, for about a hundred years, a religious, mystical, and spiritual melting pot. In the mid-ninth century, however, a fundamentalist Taoist emperor took over (sounds like an oxymoron, doesn't it?) and outlawed all other religions, even Buddhism. Things changed again later, of course, as they tended to do along the Silk Road.

Without further ado . . .

The Fate of the Hunchback

Once upon a time, there was a hunchback from Samarqand who worked for the Chinese imperial court in Ch'ang-an. He was, in fact, the favorite jester of the emperor. Now, you may think that this poor hunchback was unfortunate to have people laughing at him all the time. However, in those days, employment opportunities did not abound for someone who was, so to speak, vertically challenged and with a hump. Hunchbacks often found work in courts during this time, throughout the Middle East and all along the Silk Road to China.

This hunchback was a real professional. He dressed in an unusual costume, a motley of many colors that he had bought in the bazaar in Istanbul. His round hat with a flat top, embroidered in gold silk, came from his hometown in Samarqand, far to the west of Ch'ang-an in central Asia. He had learned both the tambourine and drum and didn't have a bad voice, either. When the jokes ran out, he could always sing a song and accompany himself.

Some years ago, he had traveled with a caravan to Ch'ang-an looking for work, since he heard that the Chinese emperor had an insatiable thirst for exotic entertainment, especially if it had an esoteric connection. So our hunchback developed a specialty: he could not only sing and tell jokes in rhyming couplets, but also give the day's astrological forecast set to music. This made him unique and, to the emperor, priceless.

We now switch our view to a Chinese tailor and his wife. One evening they were returning from a pleasant evening at the local tavern. It was their wedding anniversary, so they were in particularly good humor and not ready to call it a night. As they neared home, they passed the hunchback, who was just returning home from court and still dressed in his finest costume. He was playing the tambourine and singing, practicing tomorrow's astrological forecast so that he could get the rhythm and tempo just right.

"Let's invite this hunchback home for a late supper," said the tailor to his wife. "He seems already very happy—and very accomplished—and could entertain us. It would be our own private party!"

The hunchback was, in fact, very happy, having been served some of the best of the imperial wine earlier that evening. He accepted the tailor's offer at once, since he could practice before a live audience. It never hurt to perfect one's craft!

When they arrived home, the tailor ordered out for some very tasty dried fish and more wine—perfect for a late evening snack. By candlelight, the tailor and his wife sat eating and listening to the hunchback, whom they plied with as much food and drink as he liked. As the night wore on, everyone became even happier.

After a particularly good song, the tailor exclaimed,

"Oh, that was the best, my jolly friend! You are truly the greatest entertainer in the world! Here, for that you need another piece of fish."

He drunkenly placed a piece of fish in the hunchback's mouth. It was a very large piece. Because it wouldn't fit, the tailor pushed a bit. He had, however, due to spatial disorientation because of too much wine, overestimated the size of the hunchback's mouth in relation to his throat. The hunchback began to choke, and despite everything the couple tried (more wine?), the piece of fish was stuck. The hunchback fell over unconscious and stopped breathing.

"Argh! You've killed him!" cried the tailor's wife. "Now what do we do?"

Both sobered up quickly and devised a plan. They would carry the hunchback secretly to the home of the

Jewish doctor and alchemist in the next street. Looking out the window they saw no one, but to be sure they wrapped the hunchback in a blanket and, as they carried him down the street, said loudly to each other things like:

"Oh, our poor little son! He fell ill suddenly and we need to take him to the doctor."

"Yes, poor lad!"

It was not very convincing, and they also didn't have a son, but if someone looked out the window or they passed by some stranger, it might be good enough. It would have to be.

The Jewish Doctor and His Wife

When they came to the home of the Jewish doctor, they had to walk up two flights of stairs to reach his door. With the hunchback's hat pulled down over his face, the tailor and his wife wedged him upright between them. Then the tailor knocked on the door.

"Who's there?" asked the doctor's wife, peeking through a crack.

"This poor man we found on the street was taken ill suddenly and we need your help! We're sorry it's so late, but we don't think he'll make it to the morning."

"Wait a moment," said the Jewish doctor's wife.

She went back into the bedroom, where her husband was reading in bed.

"Another emergency. Do you want to go or not? They could always go somewhere else. It's very late."

"Oh, all right," said the Jewish doctor. "The Torah enjoins us to help the helpless, and we do live on the good will of our patients here in China."

In the meantime, the tailor and his wife had propped the hunchback up against the door and scurried away home. When the doctor opened the door, the hunchback fell down the two flights of stairs. The doctor ran after him.

"What's all this commotion?" asked his wife, who had come to the door.

"This hunchback is dead," replied her husband. "I'm afraid I've killed him. Who were those people who brought him?"

"No idea, it's very dark by our door," said his wife. "What do we do now?"

"Hmm. I suggest we take him to the home of the Muslim cleaner a few doors away. He's usually out late at work. He can deal with him."

That's what they did.

Now some homes in Ch'ang-an had flat, partially open roofs, with shafts for ventilation. One could easily access a roof from a neighboring roof. After carrying the hunchback across the rooftops, the doctor and his wife used ropes to lower him through one of the shafts into the Muslim cleaner's kitchen. They left him slumped against a wall and then went back home to bed.

"We'll say nothing more about it," said the doctor. "We can't let word get out that I accidentally killed one of my patients."

The Muslim Cleaner

A few hours later, in the middle of the night, the cleaner returned home from a round of jobs. He primarily cleaned for the imperial court, and as with modern offices today, the best time to clean was the middle of the night when most of the rooms were unoccupied.

Our cleaner was obsessive about cleaning, which is why he was a good one. However, due to his being out late most nights, he had a problem in his own kitchen with rats, which were always getting into his grain. He couldn't very well leave a candle lit while he was out—it would be a fire hazard. He had cleaned and cleaned, but they were obviously coming in from the outside, so he set traps. There was nothing more he could do.

When he came into the kitchen that night, it was very dark, with only a little light from the moon shining in through one of the roof shafts. He suddenly stopped, seeing a small, shadowy figure against the wall. Grabbing a large wooden spoon on the table, he attacked the figure, giving it one heavy blow on the head.

"Take that, you thief! And here I thought it was rats!"

The figure at once fell over. Lighting a lantern, the cleaner inspected.

"Oh-oh," he said. The cleaner recognized the hunchback from the palace.

Thinking quickly, he carried him over his shoulder into the marketplace. Thank Allah, there was no one on the street at that time of night. He propped the hunchback up in a dark corner and ran away.

The Christian Broker

Now, without overly lengthening this part of the story, it does all happen again. The dark corner chosen by the Muslim cleaner was just outside the shop of a Christian broker. Like today, a broker in those days was someone who bought goods wholesale from caravans and sold them at a higher price to buyers traveling further east in China.

The broker had returned home very late from a party, and he was almost completely drunk. He was on top of the hunchback before he noticed and fell right on top of him. Thinking he was an assailant or a thief, he instinctively pushed him down and sat on top of him. Then he noticed he wasn't breathing.

At that very moment, the night watch happened to come around the corner.

"Here, here! What's going on?" he cried, running over.

"This little person . . . was in the corner near my shop . . . I fell over him. Maybe I pushed him or hit him. I don't remember!" babbled the broker incoherently.

"You've killed this little man, for sure," said the watch. "And if his clothing is anything to go by, he's a court retainer. You're in big trouble."

Lifting the hunchback over his shoulder, the watch arrested the Christian broker and escorted him back to headquarters. His boss directed him to take the broker and the body to the imperial court. There the guard recognized the hunchback and took the broker to jail to await the judge in the morning. This was now only a few hours away. Two other guards lay the hunchback gently on a plank of wood and carried him to a side room. They would need to tell the emperor as soon as he awoke.

The next morning, when informed, the emperor was very sad and angry. He overrode any judicial procedure (which wasn't very much in any case) and ordered the broker to be executed in the main square that morning. The emperor felt he would need to make an example of someone who attacked imperial employees, especially someone as good humored and professional as his personal jester. How could the poor man have had any enemies?

The Proposed Execution

The execution ceremony took place on a platform in the main square. People gathered around, since this was a regular occurrence. Probably another vizier, they thought. A court official with a loud voice announced what the broker had done and whom he had killed. Guards led the broker up the steps to the chopping block, where the executioner was waiting.

"Have any last words, last prayers, anything like that?" the executioner asked.

"I know I'm guilty," said the broker to the crowd, "but it was an accident! I don't think I hit him that hard. May Jesus have mercy on me!"

It just so happened that at that moment, the Muslim cleaner was passing through the square on his way to do some shopping. When he heard the announcement, he had pangs of conscience. The Qur'an says that if you kill one person, it is as if you kill all of humanity, he thought. Here it was coming true. He didn't want two persons' deaths on his soul on the Day of Judgment.

"Wait!" he called out, "this man is innocent. I killed the hunchback!"

"What's that? You did?" exclaimed the captain of the guard. Consulting his fellow officers, they decided to simply replace the broker with the cleaner. The emperor wanted someone executed that morning, after all. They set it all up again, along with the announcement and last words.

"*Estaferallah* (forgive me, Allah)!" said the cleaner to the crowd. "I thought he was someone robbing food in my kitchen."

And yes, at that moment, the Jewish doctor and his wife also walked by, just as the second announcement and confession were being made. "This is bad," said the doctor to his wife. "My neighbor–and me responsible. I can't live with that and call myself a healer. What would Moses do?" His wife reluctantly agreed.

"Wait!" he cried out.

The procedure was repeated.

Just as they were about to execute the doctor, of course, the tailor and his wife arrived. They also wanted to make a clean breast of things. And that left the captain of the guard in a quandary. He interrogated them all briefly.

"You can't *all* have killed him!" said the captain accusingly. "First, he's too small. Second, you were all in different locations. I'd better take you all to the emperor."

Only about an hour had gone by for all this to unfold. When the captain of the guard arrived back at the palace, the emperor expected him to simply say the execution had gone off routinely. Instead, here he was dragging the broker back in along with five other people.

Now the emperor wanted to honor the hunchback at an imperial court funeral later that afternoon. The guards had placed his body on a small string bed leaning against the wall next to the emperor's throne. Invitations for the wake had already gone out, and the emperor had booked various priests, monks, alchemists, and assorted holy people in his entourage to offer farewell prayers and benedictions. The failure of the execution was a major hitch in his plans.

"What's all this, then?" demanded the emperor impatiently. "Some problem?"

"They *all* say they killed him, sire," replied the guard. "But it's impossible!"

"Explain yourselves," demanded the emperor.

And at that point they told him their stories, pretty much as I've told you.

A Saving Story

"An incredible story," said the emperor, shaking his head. Court employees came and went, of course. They usually either died of natural causes or were carried off to the square to meet their maker at the emperor's direction. Having a mordant sense of humor, the emperor decided on an unusual solution.

"This beloved hunchback," he said, gesturing toward the little man leaning against the wall, "was my favorite entertainer. He devoted his life to telling stories and singing songs, including the daily astrological forecast, of course. So I make the following ruling. If any of you can tell me a better story than the one you just told, I will spare the lot of you. It needs to be a true, verifiable story. If no one has a good story, then you all die in recompense for the hunchback."

The group blanched in unison and looked at one another.

"Great emperor!" said the Christian broker. "I've lived a boring life. This is the most bizarre thing that has ever happened to me. I don't have any such story."

The Muslim cleaner and the Jewish doctor and his wife also made their apologies and looked down hopelessly.

They were just about ready to give up, when the Chinese tailor piped up.

"My emperor, I may have a story that tops this."

"Let's hear it," said the emperor. The others looked on with desperate hope in their eyes.

"It didn't actually happen to me," said the tailor, "but I heard it yesterday from a man to whom it did, a fellow tailor. Let me explain.

"Yesterday was my wife's and my wedding anniversary. I had intended to be home early so that we could have a long, festive evening, but I was delayed at my tailors' guild meeting. That's why we were out so late and met the hunchback coming home."

"Okay," said the emperor, "and the interesting part is?"

"Patience please, sire," said the tailor, licking his lips nervously.

"We were delayed at the meeting, because we were honoring a visiting tailor from Isfahan in Persia. He had recently moved to Ch'ang-an, so we were initiating him into our guild and telling him our rules. For these occasions, we always throw a party with wine, food, and entertainment, especially when the colleague hails from far away. The Persian tailor was a young man who did excellent work. But he had suffered some sort of unfortunate accident, because he walked with a terrible limp.

"The party was going splendidly. As part of the celebration, we invited in a barber to groom anyone who wanted a quick shave or haircut. No sooner had this bald barber entered the room than the young Persian tailor became pale, then his face flushed and he stomped out of the room. We had to coax him back to tell us what the matter was. At first, he was unwilling to say, but we all prevailed on him.

"Here is the story that the Persian tailor told us."

A Haircut Gone Wrong

At this point, as you can see, the stories within stories begin. Telling these live, one simply changes one's voice or expression. It's done in three or four dimensions. Presenting the story on a flat page calls for us to burst the confines of traditional grammar and the rules of "point of view." In order not to confuse the reader with multiple quote marks, which buzz around the brain like pesky flies, I have simplified things. The Persian tailor takes over the story from me for this part.

This barber! He's the devil in disguise! He's the reason my leg is permanently damaged. I ran away from Isfahan to escape him, and now I find him here, thousands of miles away, just when I thought I was safe!

Colleagues, listen to my story: one day I was returning from work, walking down one of the small lanes in Isfahan, when I happened to glance up at an open window of a building that obviously was owned by someone important. At the window appeared a young woman who just happened to have her veil down. I was stunned. She was the most beautiful creature I had ever seen! Without delay I decided to find out who she was.

Having made inquiries, I found out that she was the daughter of a local religious judge—and not just any judge, but the most fanatical in Isfahan. He interpreted all sorts of penalties into the Qur'an that aren't there by quoting this or that obscure authority, who was probably just as angry and unhappy as he was. My friends urged me to give up my quest. The judge would never allow me to see his daughter, much less talk to her, and even speaking about betrothal was out of the question. I am not very religious, although I try to remember God's Unity and treat others fairly. To me that's the whole of religion. Anyway, I'm also of the wrong social class, just a poor tailor. In other words, no hope.

But I refused to give up. Every day I loitered near the same window of the judge's house, hoping to catch a glimpse of my beloved. In my own mind, I was already calling her that. My beloved! At last, one day she opened the window again and seeing me, smiled.

"I recognize you from the other day," she said coolly. "Why are you hanging around our house?"

"'Yes, it is me!" I replied, bowing deeply to her. "I am your most humble, abject slave and would do anything to spend some time with you. Like a bee attracted to honey, I am hopelessly circling around you, my flower." It wasn't very good, but I figured that I needed to work fast and make my pitch. Judging from the position of the sun, her father might arrive home any moment.

"Okay," she said, looking at me seductively. "Come back tomorrow about midday. It's Friday and my father will be at juma (the midday communal prayers) most of the afternoon. I'll be waiting." Then she closed the shutters abruptly.

I was, as you can imagine, overjoyed. I decided to tell no one, since I didn't want anything to spoil the fulfillment of my dreams. Who knew . . . perhaps we could run away together to the east along the Silk Road?

The next morning, I bathed and then called in at a barber to have my hair and beard trimmed. I wanted to look my best. And that is where this beast enters the story.

At first things went fine. The barber began to cut my hair, and we talked casually about the weather, as you do with barbers. Then he went on to other things.

"You know," he said, "I am also a famous astrologer, as well as an alchemist, a healer, a geomancer, and a dowser."

"Mmm-hmm," I mumbled. By this time, he had lathered and begun to shave me, even though he hadn't finished cutting my hair. I thought I should just respond with something but not give him too much encouragement. Time was passing.

"Yes!" he continued, "perhaps you'd like to take advantage of one of my other services? Because I like you, it won't cost any extra."

"Not today," I replied quickly. "But maybe another time."

"Now really," he said, "how can you turn down an offer like this?" He stopped shaving me and went into the back room. He brought back an astrolabe and a small book.

"I can already see here," said the barber, looking in the book, "as well as from the shape of your head and its various bumps—I am also a renowned physiognamist, you know—that this could be an auspicious day for you."

He poked his head out the window and sighted through the astrolabe into the sky.

"But there could be dangerous factors," he said, turning back to me and wagging his finger. "What are you planning for the rest of the day?"

"Nothing really," I said. I wanted him to get back to shaving me, and I certainly didn't want to tell him that I intended to woo the daughter of Isfahan's most conservative judge.

"I can't believe it!" he said. He went into the back room again, rummaged around noisily, and brought out a box full of some smooth stones with various markings on them. He played with the stones awhile, then he tossed a few, one at a time, onto a nearby table. He announced, "I'll bet you're going to woo a young lady!"

My heart sank.

"No, I said, "I just want my hair and beard trimmed! And you're only half finished with both. Can you get on with it, please? I only have limited time!"

"So you do have some appointment! Tell me. What is it?"

I made up something quickly.

"I have friends coming by for lunch, and I have to get in food and wine and prepare things."

"Oh, in that case, I'll come with you. I'm also an excellent chef. I'd love to meet some new friends."

"No, that won't be possible; it's a closed gathering, a sort of political meeting about our guild business."

"I was once political adviser to the ruler of the city. I could help!"

"No, no!" I protested. "Can't you just finish my hair and beard? Look! I'll supply you with the same food that my friends and I are going to eat. I'll just save some from our gathering and bring it by later. Now would you please hurry!"

"I'm sure you're holding something back," he said, swinging a pendulum over me. "Are you sure you're not meeting a woman?"

Then I heard the call to midday prayer. It was time for juma, and the judge would be leaving home. However, I couldn't get this devil of a barber to finish with me. He kept coming up with this or that offer to help solve all my life's problems. It went on for some time, and I became desperate. Finally, I bolted out of the chair and out the door, wiping the soap off my face onto my robe as I ran down the street. By the sun, it was already a half hour into juma. The prayer would be over and the sermon would be starting. I ran faster and arrived at the judge's house in a sweaty, disheveled state. Catching my breath, I saw the barber appearing around the corner behind me.

"I used to be a champion runner!" he said. "I thought so, this is some secret tryst!"

"Go away! I don't want you! I don't need you!" I yelled at him. The barber walked away, and when he had gone back around the corner, I knocked on the door.

"What took you so long?" asked the judge's daughter as she opened the door. "And what kind of state are in you in? Half-shaven! Who do you think I am, some common tart?"

"I apologize! I apologize, my dearest. There was an emergency. If I told you, you wouldn't believe it," I said. We went inside and up the stairs to her room. But just as we were closing the door, we heard the judge out in the street calling up to his daughter's open window:

"I'm home early, my daughter! The juma talk was unusually short and not very inspiring. Most of my friends and I went home early. I hope you've been behaving while I was away!" Then we also heard another voice in the street, one that I knew only too well.

"Excuse me, sir, but this can't be your house. My master has just gone inside to meet his lover. So please don't disturb them!"

"Your master?" exploded the judge. "What! Who are you? I'll kill him! No, first I'll have his hands and feet cut off legally, then I'll kill him, then I'll stone him just to make sure!"

At this point, his daughter and I panicked. There was nowhere to hide—not even the usual large chest that occupies young women's rooms, primarily to hide their lovers. And anyway, the barber had given me away, so there was no hope. There was nothing for it, so as the judge came up the stairs, I jumped out of the window. As I landed I felt excruciating pain in my leg, but I kept on running. Better that than be cut apart or stoned or whatever. Down the street after me came the demon barber.

"Wait! I can heal you!"

I turned around, knocked him down, and kept on running until I lost him. Not even going back home for my clothes or tools, I found a caravan going east and left at once. And I didn't stop until I came here.

The Actual Barber

"That was the story that the young Persian tailor told us, sire," reported the Chinese tailor to the emperor. "And then we had to confirm it with the barber, who wanted to talk about everything else, of course, and read our palms and whatnot. Finally, I had to tear myself away to meet my wife. But my guild secretary knows where the young tailor lives—and the barber, too!"

"It's a remarkable story," said the emperor, "but is it really true? Can there really be a person like this barber in my city? Guards! Go to the tailors' guild secretary, take the directions that he gives you, and fetch this incredible barber, if he exists."

The six potential execution victims waited anxiously. The emperor whiled away the time playing backgammon with one of his courtiers. Finally, they brought in a bald man who strode into the room as if he owned it.

"That's him!" cried the tailor.

"We have been hearing a story about you," said the emperor smoothly. "Can you confirm it?" And the emperor then retold the story more or less as I've told you.

"Well, honored emperor," replied the barber, "as I am new to your city, I may not understand all of your beautiful, foreign ways as well as I might. In the main, the general outline of what you've related has the shadow of a resemblance to something that may have happened to me. I am, of course, a very skilled healer, astrologer, geomancer, alchemist, phrenologist, palm reader, rune reader, master chef, athletic coach, and political adviser, as well as a barber, in case you have any need.

"However, in at least one point, the story is completely wrong. I am not talkative. I am the soul of brevity, in fact. In my family, I am known as the 'silent one.' I could tell you the story of my six brothers, who are really very talkative."

Here, without any encouragement, the barber went on to tell the stories of his six brothers, each of which was at least as long as this one so far. Really!

"But me, no," he concluded, "you will always hear a brief, straight answer from me."

"You are not talkative?" asked the emperor, tears of laughter streaming down his face.

"My liege, I can assure you!" said the barber, and here he began to walk proudly around the room, looking at all of the decorations. "I can see that you are used to the finest of everything here, and in the few days I've been in your city I've been very impressed with all I've seen. However, even in the most perfect of empires there is always room for improvement. To stand still is death, right? Now a person of my abilities could be of great usefulness, especially. . . ." At this point, the barber was standing just in front of the body of the hunchback, propped against the wall.

"Especially as I am the tersest, the most truthful man in the whole wide world!" Here he opened his arms wide in a quick, forceful gesture. Now it just so happened that one of his elbows went backward and caught the hunchback under the sternum in just the right place. A piece of fish flew out of the hunchback's mouth and across the room, almost hitting the emperor, who ducked just in time. The hunchback coughed once, and the color began to return to his face. He looked around in astonishment. How did he get back to the palace, and who were all these people?

"Here now, what's wrong with this little fellow?" asked the barber, who hadn't really noticed him before. "Thought he was very quiet. Ah, I see! I was just in time! As I told you, healing is one of my specialties. Especially healing those who are vertically challenged."

The emperor at once released the tailor and his wife, the Jewish doctor and his wife, the Muslim cleaner, and the Christian broker. He sent them all home with a warning, but also a few presents, too, since it had been an entertaining day. While all of this was going on, the barber continued to talk as if nothing else were happening.

"Why are you all laughing there? Healing is a serious art! I'll have you know that I studied medicine in Baghdad with the greatest and best of my generation. . . ."

The emperor just shook his head and turned to the hunchback.

"Welcome back from the dead, my friend! You will have some competition from now on, you see? Do you have an astrological forecast for tomorrow?"

IX

Reversals of Fortune

Like all folk traditions of the world, Sufi stories abound with tales of "reversal of fortune." The rich become poor, the poor become rich. What seems to be good luck turns out bad, and vice versa.

Many of our popular films—from *The Treasure of the Sierra Madre* to *Trading Places*—seem to be based on such stories.

A Sufi might say that there is something in our soul—the part of us already connected 24/7 to the Mystery behind the cosmos—that intuitively knows unity. The personal self, trying to appropriate this wordless experience for itself, always looks for the same balance of opposites in outer circumstances. Sometimes we search for this balance in healthy ways, sometimes in unhealthy ones.

These two stories from Turkey show different sides of the "reversal" theme. In the first, a certain persistence (albeit with reluctance in the beginning), combined with skills or habits already developed, propels the protagonist forward. Although this type of story can end badly (as in Pushkin's story of the fisherman and the magic fish), this one works out very nicely for everyone. The second story is one of my favorites of this type; although you think you know where it's going, the storytellers created an interesting twist at the end.

How Difficult Can Astrology Be?

The cobbler Hassan could have happily repaired shoes in old Istanbul until Allah called him to his eternal rest. In fact, he might easily have done so, except for an insignificant occurrence, which to the casual observer might seem to be mere chance. But there is also what some people call *kismet*, or fate, to consider.

It just so happened that one day, while Hassan's wife Fatima was at the local *hamam*, the women's bath and sauna, she was interrupted. The wife of the chief astrologer to the sultan needed a private compartment and there were none available. The attendants quickly estimated the pecking order and judged Fatima to be on the lowest rung. They booted her out unceremoniously, without even giving her the customary massage. She arrived home very angry. She told her husband the story and concluded:

"Hassan, I won't have this anymore. I want *you* to become the chief astrologer to the sultan. After all, how difficult can astrology be?"

Hassan tried to argue with his wife. What he knew was leather, and stitching, and repairing things. He didn't know anything about the stars, and he really had no interest in them. What Allah wished to happen, would happen. Why try to predict one's fate or argue with it?

Fatima, however, was insistent. She was confident that Hassan could do better.

"Just try!" she said. "Maybe you have a talent you don't know about. Stop what you're doing right now. We have a little money saved. Buy what you need to become an astrologer. Then go to the bazaar and see who comes along."

Wanting to preserve peace in the family, Hassan did this. Having consulted a friend in the market, he bought an astrolabe (even though he didn't know how to use it) and some scrolls with charts listing the positions of the stars during the year. Then he went to the astrologer-and-seer's area of the bazaar and sat down on a rug he had brought from home. He started to fiddle with the astrolabe and soon became completely confused. He looked at all the numbers on the charts with even less comprehension. He had never needed any mathematics to make or repair a shoe and so had never learned any. Finally, he laid everything aside, sighed, and gazed up into the sky.

It just so happened that at that moment one of the many princesses of the sultan's palace happened to be passing by, looking for an astrologer. She hadn't seen this one before. Instead of fiddling with charts and gadgets as most of the others did, he was gazing meditatively into the sky. He must have some deeper knowledge!

"You simply *must* help me!" she said, rushing up to him and sitting down. "I lost my diamond ring at the *hamam*. It's very important that I find it!"

Hassan was in despair. What could he say? He sighed again, gazed into the sky, and then looked at the princess. He was just about to decline when his practiced eye noticed a small rip in the side of her pantaloons. They really needed a bit of stitching. Involuntarily, he said, "I see a small tear. . . ."

"A tear! A crack! Yes! That's it!" exclaimed the princess. "I remember now. I left my ring in a small crack in the stone bank near the cold pool. It must still be there!"

She rushed off back to the *hamam* and, sure enough, the ring was there. She was overjoyed. Being an honorable princess, she at once returned to Hassan and gave him several gold pieces as payment.

Hassan packed up and returned home. It was a good day's work, if one could call it work. He had earned more than he would have made as a cobbler. He reported the results to his wife.

"Look," he said, "I was lucky this time, but that doesn't mean I should continue. Let's call it quits while we're ahead."

"Not a chance," replied his wife. "It's a sign that you have a talent and should continue. Try once more again tomorrow."

As it so happened, the princess of the (formerly) lost ring was very talkative. Since gossip was the main currency of value in the sultan's harem, soon everyone at the palace was talking about the miraculous ability of Hassan the Astrologer as a "finder."

This came to the attention of the sultan himself, who, it just so happened, had lost one of his favorite gold chains, one inlaid with diamonds. He had already tried all his other court astrologers without any luck, so he decided to try Hassan. Accompanied by various retainers, he visited Hassan at his home.

"I've heard good things about you, Hassan," said the sultan. "While you seem to be new to astrology, you've had some remarkable success. Of course, the penalty for posing as an astrologer when you really aren't one is very severe. Your head, probably. But we won't speak of this. Now, can you find my golden chain inlaid with diamonds?"

Hassan was again in despair. What could he do? To put off the inevitable, he asked the sultan how many diamonds the chain contained. Twenty-four, replied the sultan. Gazing into the sky, Hassan said that in that case he would need twenty-four hours to solve the mystery. The sultan and his retinue left.

Unknown to Hassan, one of the many wives of the sultan had become obsessed with the king's necklace and had stolen it. She had sent one of her handmaidens to listen under the window at Hassan and Fatima's house during the sultan's visit. The handmaiden lingered a bit after the royal party left, to hear what Hassan might say.

"Woman, woman!" said Hassan to his wife. "What evil spirit impelled you to this path, dragging others along with you? When twenty-four hours are up, you will repent. But it will be too late. Your husband will be gone, and you won't have even a hope of uniting with him in paradise!"

Hassan was, of course, referring to himself and his wife. The handmaiden, however, not being able to see him, thought that he was talking about her mistress. She hurried back to the palace and reported Hassan's words verbatim to the sultan's wife. The wife panicked. This was her worst nightmare. She at once ran off to appeal to Hassan in person.

Having been admitted, she plopped down in front of Hassan and prostrated herself. "You don't know me, wise Hodja, but please have compassion on my weakness. I will pray for you at least five times a day. Please don't expose me to the anger of my husband. I will do anything you ask!"

Hassan did not, in fact, have any idea what this strange woman was talking about.

"What Allah has decreed will happen, no matter what I do. How can I help you?" He looked at her meaningfully, hoping she would reveal more.

"If you won't help me, then I will have to go and confess to the sultan. Maybe he will forgive me!" She fingered something that looked like a chain around her neck, hidden underneath the folds of her gown.

Hassan, used to noticing small details, then understood. "I must consult the stars," he said and gazed into the heavens as if for an answer. Well, it had worked before. He waited.

"Will the answer come before twenty-four hours are up?" asked the sultan's wife in desperation. "Shall I give you the chain now? You could give it to the sultan without any explanation, couldn't you?"

Hassan realized that this wouldn't work, since the sultan would demand to know where he had gotten it. He told the sultan's wife that, in return for a modest fee, he promised not to reveal her theft. The condition was that she had to promise to return to the palace and place the chain between the top and bottom mattresses of the sultan's bed.

When the sultan arrived the next day, Hassan told him that the stars had decreed that, if he wanted both the chain and thief, it would take a very long time. If he wanted only the necklace, the stars could satisfy him immediately. What could the sultan say? He would be very happy to have the diamond chain again.

Hassan then told him to go back to the palace and look between the mattresses of his bed. The sultan rushed away and found the chain, just as described. Then he returned to Hassan and rewarded him with ten times more gold than the princess had given him originally. In addition, Hassan's reputation as the "astrologer of the moment" increased exponentially. The sultan's wife also returned later and rewarded Hassan handsomely.

Hassan again begged his wife to allow him to stop. She refused. Hassan continued, using the method that, when asked a question, he would gaze into the sky and then say the first thing that came into his mind. Or if he heard nothing, he would say that the stars declined to speak on the subject in question.

As these stories go, there is usually a "third time," and so here it is.

Forty cases of gold went missing from the sultan's treasury. It was a prodigious heist, and neither the court detectives nor the court astrologers could offer any clue as to where the missing gold had gone. Even the chief astrologer was in disgrace. So, the sultan again turned to Hassan.

This time Hassan thought he was doomed. What would the punishment be for failure, for posing falsely as an astrologer? Exile? Death? Since there were forty cases of gold, Hassan asked the Sultan for forty days to solve the mystery.

Now, as mentioned, Hassan was not exactly innumerate, but he was mathematically challenged. He had no concrete idea of what "forty" meant. He normally fixed one shoe at a time and was not much for multitasking. So he went to the market and asked the shopkeeper for forty dried chickpeas.

He knew it would be useless to complain to his wife about the seriousness of their plight, but he decided to try anyway, using the chickpeas as an illustrative prop.

"Forty cases of gold, forty days, forty men, forty lives, forty. . . ." he said, rambling incoherently to his wife, taking one of the forty beans out of a small pouch and showing it to her. "And here is one of them. The rest remain in their place until the day of reckoning."

Unknown to Hassan, the band of thieves who had stolen the gold (who happened to be forty in number) had heard of the sultan's plan to consult the famous astrologer. They had sent one of their number to spy on him. Because of Hassan's reputation, they needed to know as soon as possible if they had been discovered.

Listening under the window, the thief heard the words "and here is one of them," and believed that Hassan had detected his presence. He quickly ran back to his gang and reported. They were very upset and decided to send another member of their band to listen again the following evening. The thief had not been waiting under the window for long when he heard Hassan say, "Forty . . . forty. And here is another of them!" as he took the next chickpea out of the bag—meaning of course, one less day left in his life.

After the spy reported, the thieves sent a delegation to Hassan, confessing the crime and offering to return the forty cases of gold at once if only he would not betray them.

Hassan was now becoming more confident in this business. He told the thieves that he had no wish to see them all executed. He promised not to reveal their involvement if they (a) buried the cases in a spot he chose, and (b) paid him a generous fee.

When the forty days were up, Hassan went to the palace and told the sultan that the stars had again spoken in the way they had concerning his chain. Perhaps this was the sultan's *kismet*? The stars said that they would reveal either the thieves or the gold, but not both. Which would it be? Forty cases of gold had greatly depleted the treasury, so the sultan immediately chose the gold. Hassan led the sultan and his servants to the location where the thieves had buried the gold. And—hurrah!—rejoicing erupted around the palace. Astrologer Hassan had done it again!

What could the sultan do? He appointed Hassan as the new chief astrologer. What could Hassan do? Well, only accept, although under the condition that the stars had told him that they had limited his powers and that he should retire soon (with a full pension, of course). So, Fatima also got her wish, at least in terms of the pecking order at the local *hamam*. She agreed that Hassan could retire as a full-time astrologer whenever he wanted, since they now had plenty of money on which to live. Hassan himself planned to become something even more unique—a famous, retired astrologer, who repaired shoes for the joy of it.

One day not too long after the case of the forty thieves, the sultan was walking with Chief Astrologer Hassan in the palace gardens. As a joke, the sultan turned away from him and grabbed a passing grasshopper in his hand.

"What do I have in my hand, Hassan? Come on, use your gifts!"

Hassan gazed into the sky. The first thing that came into his mind was an old Turkish proverb about the precariousness of human life, which he repeated to the sultan:

"Your Majesty! The grasshopper never knows where its third leap will take it!"

The sultan was so impressed that he never tested Hassan again, even in jest. And Hassan concluded that astrology was not, after all, so difficult.

Hadji Ahmed's Dream

During the time of the Ottoman Empire, an old scrap metal collector and his wife lived on the shores of the Sea of Marmara in Turkey. In case you don't know that part of the world, the Sea of Marmara connects the Aegean Sea on the west, which is the gateway to Europe, with the Black Sea on the east, the gateway to Asia. As such, the sea was and still is a strategic passageway. To defend it, the Ottomans built tall towers along the shoreline to overlook it. Cannons above, poor people living below. That was the way of things, then and now.

Our scrap metal collector, Hadji Ahmed, lived in one of these towers with his wife Kerima. Probably you know, but a "hadji" means someone who has traveled to Mecca and completed the ritual stages of the annual Hajj, or pilgrimage. (Don't confuse a *hadji* with a *hodja*, please!) For poor people, making the Hajj was a once-in-a-lifetime (at best) undertaking, and Hadji Ahmed and Kerima had sacrificed much so that they could accomplish it.

Despite the honor given to anyone who was a hadji, Ahmed could do no better for a living than to gather bits of iron and other metal debris each day and sell it to blacksmiths.

As time wore on, Hadji Ahmed became more demoralized by his lot in life.

"Ah," he thought to himself. "Here I am, a hadji. Yet all day long I'm stuck gathering this rubbish, which ends up in cannon balls, or even in the horseshoes of the rich that I see passing by me in their carriages. Worse yet, it ends up in the shoes of donkeys owned by farmers, who are still better off than I am. I can't even afford to ride a donkey, much less own one."

Ahmed fell asleep each night dreaming of wealth and comfort. But in the morning the same harsh reality dawned. Back to gathering rubbish.

He began to call on the spirit of his dreams to change things around for him. Instead of wealth at night and poverty during the day, why not the other way around—please! But for many, many nights, nothing changed.

Then one night, he heard a voice in his dreams saying emphatically, "Go to Egypt! It shall all be as you wish!" The message comforted him by day and inspired him even more at night. The voice in the dream repeated the message night after night, and Ahmed became obsessed by it.

For instance, one day Kerima asked him, "Ahmed, did you bring home any bread this evening?" Ahmed replied,

"No, tomorrow, I'll go tomorrow." He had, of course, brought the bread, but he thought his wife had asked, "Ahmed, have you gone to Egypt yet?"

He began to talk incessantly about the idea with his friends and neighbors, who quickly became tired of the theme.

"Poor Ahmed," they said, "he's gone around the bend, we fear!"

"Been working so hard, all that heavy lifting!"

"Perhaps metal poisoning?"

One morning when he woke up, he went to Kerima and said, "That's it. I'm going. I'm going to the land of wealth! Wish me well."

Kerima was shocked. She thought it was only a fantasy Ahmed had developed and that he would get over it. As he went out the door, she wailed and wrung her hands. The neighbors heard the racket and tried to comfort her. But it was too late to stop Hadji Ahmed; he had already left.

He went straight to the harbor and found a ship bound for Alexandria. He told the captain that a voice in a dream had instructed him to go to Egypt, and so the captain simply had to take him, even though he had no money. As it so happened, the captain was a superstitious yet honorable man who believed that he should give anyone who was either holy or half-witted free passage wherever they wanted. This Ahmed had to be one or both, so the captain agreed and took him all the way to Alexandria.

It was a journey of many months. When Ahmed reached Alexandria, he wandered around the town, always expecting someone to offer him the wealth his dream had promised him. But people contributed only a few scraps of bread, which barely kept him alive. After some weeks, he wandered south to Cairo. But nothing changed.

After some months, he grew increasingly weak, and what's worse, increasingly tired of life. He decided to ask Allah to allow him to die. The best place to do this seemed to be at the pyramids. Someone had told him that many people were already buried there.

Hadji Ahmed went to Giza and began to ask aloud—as a formal petition—that Allah allow the stones to have compassion and fall on him, right then and there. He made his petition loudly and, of course, in Turkish.

It just so happened that a young Turkish man who had emigrated to Egypt was passing by. He heard Ahmed wailing and complaining to Allah.

"My father, why such despair? Can life really be so bad? Is your soul suffering so much that you would commit a sin by killing yourself rather than endure your prescribed time in the body?"

"My son," replied Ahmed mournfully, "far away in Turkey, I lived by gathering scrap metal, a junkman. I could feed my wife and myself that way. I came to Egypt because a voice in a dream told me I would find wealth and comfort here. But things are even worse. I am alone and destitute, dying of starvation. And all of this because of a dream!"

"My father, poor you! I sympathize with you. But surely you should know that you shouldn't allow a dream to lead you so far from your family and friends. Aren't the bonds of love and affinity worth something, even though we can't count them in coins? I mean, I also have such dreams. I dream every night that I see a great wall connected to many tall towers, on the shore of the sea of Marmara. I see an old man and woman living in one of these towers, near a large, ancient oak tree. It has seven branches and its trunk is so large that it would need four men, hands joined, to reach around it. Every night, the old man in the dream tells me to dig under this tree and I will find a treasure. But do I go back there? No, I am not such a fool as to risk everything on a dream! My life here is good. Take my advice and follow my example. Give up this nonsense and return to hearth and home."

"You *have* encouraged me. Allah be praised!" exclaimed Hadji Ahmed. "Yes, it was only a dream but you have interpreted it. I will return!"

The two parted very happily. The younger man was happy that he had been able to encourage a fellow Turk and Muslim to continue living. Hadji Ahmed was overjoyed that, after much tribulation, Allah had sent a stranger to interpret his dream.

Somehow, perhaps with the same ship's captain, Hadji Ahmed returned home. He did not seem very much changed after his long absence and again took up collecting scrap metal. When his neighbors asked him about the trip, he would only say, "A dream sent me away, and a dream brought me back."

The neighbors all said, "Really, he must be some sort of holy man!"

As you might have already guessed, one night Hadji Ahmed borrowed a spade from a neighbor and went to a large, ancient oak tree with seven branches that grew near their tower. After digging a bit, he found a chest full of gold, silver, and precious gems. He buried the chest again and went home to ponder things.

Of course, the tree, the land under it, and all the towers were owned by the sultan. Unlike today, there was no such thing as "treasure trove," whereby someone finding a treasure could share the proceeds with the owner of the land or with the state. If suddenly Hadji Ahmed became rich and someone discovered where the treasure had come from, both he and his wife would be arrested as thieves. The penalty could be death. Minimally, the treasure would be confiscated. There was always a need for more cannon balls, right?

Ahmed fell asleep asking for a solution in his dreams. When he awoke in the morning, he had it. But he needed to make one test first. Should he even tell his wife what had happened?

Sneaking out of bed, he fetched an egg. Then he crept back into bed. When his wife awoke, Ahmed turned to her and said, "My dear, I'm afraid that all this running back and forth to Egypt has changed me somehow. Maybe a passing magician cast a spell on me. They have many of them in Egypt, you know." He reached underneath him. "It seems that during the night I laid this egg." He showed Kerima the egg, looking very downcast. "This is very unnatural. Please don't tell the neighbors. If they hear about it, my reputation may be ruined!"

With that, he arose, dressed, put his sack on his back, and went out for a day of collecting scrap metal.

When he returned home, he found a line of neighbors at his door.

"What's all this?" asked Hadji Ahmed.

"Now we know! Not only are you a holy man, but you have special powers. You laid a dozen eggs overnight, we heard. So, we've come for our share, of course! You *will* have more tomorrow, won't you?"

Hadji Ahmed sighed. At least that question was settled. He put "Plan B" into operation.

Every day he went out with his sack to collect scrap metal. As usual, at the end of the day, he and his wife sorted through the lot, separating what the blacksmiths would buy from any other junk.

It just so happened that one night they found a gold coin. And on subsequent nights, they found a few more gold as well as silver coins, and then a week later a precious stone.

Thereafter Ahmed and Kerima always had what they needed. And they had quite enough to share with their neighbors (including buying them eggs), who all considered themselves blessed because of Hadji Ahmed and his dream.

Wild Nature

The smell from within
that only reaches
our own noses
will all come out
at the Resurrection.

The inner being of a
human being
is wild nature, a jungle.
If you are aware of yourself as
part of the divine breath,
be very aware
when you travel inside.

Inside lurk thousands of
wolves and wild hogs,
some obedient, some less so,
some in tune with the soul,
some seriously out of touch.

The way we act depends on
who (or what) has the upper hand.
When the gold content is
more than the copper,
we tend to call the mixture "gold."

At one moment,
a wolf rises within;
at another, a lovely beloved
with a face like Joseph.

Everything connects.
Both benign and hateful qualities
pass from heart to heart
by hidden routes.

Wisdom and quality
can pass from a human being
into an ox or an ass.

A wild horse becomes tame,
a bear dances,
or a goat nods to you
in greeting.

In this way,
the heart-wishes of human beings
have passed into the dog,
so that it has become a hunter,
or a shepherd, or
a guardian of the house.

In the famous story,
the Sleepers in the Cave
passed the qualities of a seeker[1]
into the dog that watched over them
for generations.

---

1 A famous story told in Syriac Christian mysticism (and shared by Sufis). A group of devout Christian believers are being persecuted by their king. They decide to go into a cave with their dog, sealing it behind them. Generations pass and when someone finally opens the cave, the dog is still there, waiting patiently for the "seven sleepers" to awaken.

Every instant,
a new species bursts
out of the heart's doorway:
now a devil,
now an angel,
now something completely wild.

Through this wonder-filled
inner jungle,
you will find a path,
known to every fearless lion,
that leads to those great hearts
ready to ensnare our own in Unity.

O you, who are no less than a dog,
steal the pearl of transformation
from those who know the Way.

Since we came here with nothing,
and can only steal,
let's steal things that
are really valuable.

Since we must bear some load
simply for living in
the world of "two-ness,"
let's carry some baggage
for the Beloved.

—Mevlana Jelaluddin Rumi
Mathnawi, Book I, 1415–1429
Version by Neil Douglas-Klotz

A Selected Reading List of Books Containing Sufi Stories

Adler, Cyrus and Allan Ramsay. (1898). *Told in the Coffee House: Turkish Tales.* London: Macmillan Company.

Arapov, Alexey. (2007). *Khodja Nasreddin: A Great Smile of the East.* Tashkent: Sanat.

Arberry, A. J., trans. (1961). *Tales from the Masnavi.* Richmond, Surrey, England: Curzon Press.

At-Tarjumana, Aisha Abd-Rahman, trans. (1974). *The Tawasin of Mansur Al-Hallaj.* Berkeley and London: Diwan Press.

Burton, Richard F., trans. (1885). *The Book of the Thousand Nights and a Night: A Plain and Literal Translation of the Arabian Nights Entertainments.* In 16 volumes. USA: The Burton Club.

Chelkowski, Peter J., trans. (1975). *Mirror of the Invisible World: Tales from the Khamseh of Nizami*. New York: Metropolitan Museum of Art.

Darbandi, Afkham and Dick Davis, trans. (1984). *Farid ud-din Attar: The Conference of the Birds*. London: Penguin Books.

Douglas-Klotz, Neil. (2005). *The Sufi Book of Life: 99 Pathways of the Heart for the Modern Dervish*. New York: Penguin Books.

Douglas-Klotz, Neil (Saadi Shakur Chishti), Joan Chittister, and Arthur Waskow. (2006). *The Tent of Abraham: Stories of Hope and Peace for Jews, Christians and Muslims*. Boston: Beacon Press.

Eastwick, Edward B., trans. (1974). *The Rose-Garden of Shekh Muslihu'd-din Sadi of Shiraz*. London: Octagon Press.

Edwards, A. Hart, trans. (1911). *The Bustan of Sadi*. Lahore: Sh. Muhammad Ashraf.

Farzan, Massud. (1974). *The Tale of the Reed Pipe*. New York: E. P. Dutton.

Fischer, Ron. (1993). *Also sprach Mulla Nasrudin: Geschichten aus der wirklichen Welt*. München: Knauer Verlag.

Haddawy, Husain, trans. (1990). *The Arabian Nights Based on the Text of the Fourteenth-Century Syrian Manuscript Edited by Muhsin Mahdi.* New York and London: W. W. Norton & Company.

Haeri, Shaykh Fadhlalla and Muneera Haeri. (2016). *Sufi Links: Illumined Encounters.* Centurion, South Africa: Zahra Publications.

Johnson, Mansur, ed. (2015). *Big Tales: All the Stories in the 12 Volumes of the Sufi Message of Hazrat Inayat Khan.* Tucson, AZ: Einstein Academy.

Khalidi, Tarif. (2001). *The Muslim Jesus: Sayings and Stories in Islamic Literature.* Cambridge, MA: Harvard University Press.

Lorimer, D. L. R. and E. O. Lorimer. (1919). *Persian Tales: Written Down for the First Time in the Original Kermani and Bakhtiari.* London: Macmillan and Company.

Nicholson, Reynold A., trans. (1926). *The Mathnawi of Jalaluddin Rumi.* In 4 volumes. London: E. J. W. Gibb Memorial Trust.

Nicholson, Reynold A., trans. (1995). *Tales of Mystic Meaning: Selections from the Mathnawi of Jalal-ud-Din Rumi.* Oxford: Oneworld Publications.

Nott, C. S., trans. (1971). *Farid-ud-din Attar: The Conference of the Birds (Mantiq ut-Tair)*. Boulder, CO: Shambhalla.

Nurbakhsh, Javad. (1983). *Jesus in the Eyes of the Sufis*. London: Khaniqahi-Nimatullahi Publications.

Parrinder, Geoffrey. (1995). *Jesus in the Qur'an*. Oxford: Oneworld Publications.

Sanadiki, Khaled. (2000). *Legends and Narratives of Islam: The Biblical Personalities*. Chicago: Kazi Publications.

Shah, Idries. (1972). *Caravan of Dreams*. Baltimore: Penguin Books.

Thackston, Wheeler M., Jr., trans. (1997). *Tales of the Prophets (Qisas al-anbiya) by Muhammad ibn Abd Allah al-Kisai*. Chicago: Kazi Publications.

Wollaston, Arthur N., trans. (1908). *Sadi's Scroll of Wisdom: Persian and English Text*. London: John Murray.

About the Author

PHOTO BY WILLIAM A. MATHEIU

NEIL DOUGLAS-KLOTZ, PH.D. (Saadi Shakur Chishti) is a renowned writer in the fields of Middle Eastern spirituality and the translation and interpretation of the ancient Semitic languages of Hebrew, Aramaic, and Arabic. Living in Scotland, he directs the Edinburgh Institute for Advanced Learning and for many years was co-chair of the Mysticism Group of the American Academy of Religion.

A frequent speaker and workshop leader, Douglas-Klotz is the author of several books. His books on the Aramaic spirituality of Jesus include *Prayers of the Cosmos, The Hidden Gospel, Original Meditation: The Aramaic Jesus and the Spirituality of Creation,* and *Blessings of the Cosmos.* His books on a comparative view of "native" Middle Eastern spirituality include *Desert Wisdom: A Nomad's Guide to Life's Big Questions* and *The Tent of Abraham* (with Rabbi Arthur Waskow and Sr. Joan Chittister). In addition to this book, Neil has another on Sufi spirituality titled *The Sufi Book of Life: 99 Pathways of the Heart for the Modern Dervish.* His biographical collections of the works of his Sufi teachers include *Sufi Vision and Initiation* (Samuel L. Lewis) and *Illuminating the Shadow* (Moineddin Jablonski). He has also written a mystery novel set in the first-century CE Holy Land titled *A Murder at Armageddon.*

For more information about Neil's work, see the website of the Abwoon Network (*www.abwoon.org*) or his Facebook page (*www.facebook.com/AuthorNeilDouglasKlotz/*).

Hampton Roads Publishing Company

. . . FOR THE EVOLVING HUMAN SPIRIT

Hampton Roads Publishing Company publishes books on a variety of subjects, including spirituality, health, and other related topics.

For a copy of our latest trade catalog, call (978) 465-0504 or visit our distributor's website at *www.redwheelweiser.com.* You can also sign up for our newsletter and special offers by going to *www.redwheelweiser.com/newsletter/.*